International Dimensions of Marketing

Vern Terpstra
UNIVERSITY OF MICHIGAN

Lloyd C. Russow
PHILADELPHIA COLLEGE OF TEXTILES AND SCIENCE

South-Western College Publishing

an International Thomson Publishing company I(T)P®

Cincinnati • Albany • Boston • Detroit • Johannesburg • London • Madrid • Melbourne • Mexico City
New York • Pacific Grove • San Francisco • Scottsdale • Singapore • Tokyo • Toronto

Publisher: Dave Shaut
Acquisitions Editor: Steve Scoble
Developmental Editor: Mardell Toomey
Marketing Manager: Sara Woelfel
Production Editor: Marci Dechter
Manufacturing Coordinator: Dana Schwartz
Cover Design: Jennifer Mayhall
Printer: Webcom

Printed in Canada
1 2 3 4 5 6 7 8 9 10

International Thomson Publishing Europe
Berkshire House
168-173 High Holborn
London, WC1V7AA, United Kingdom

Nelson ITP, Australia
102 Dodds Street
South Melbourne
Victoria 3205 Australia

Nelson Canada
1120 Birchmount Road
Scarborough, Ontario
Canada M1K 5G4

International Thomson Publishing Southern Africa
Building 18, Constantia Square
138 Sixteenth Road, P.O. Box 2459
Halfway House, 1685 South Africa

International Thomson Editores
Seneca, 53
Colonia Polanco
11560 Mèxico D.F. Mèxico

International Thomson Publishing Asia
60 Alberta Street #15-01
Albert Complex
Singapore 189969

International Thomson Publishing Japan
Hirakawa-cho Kyowa Building, 3F
2-2-1 Hirakawa-cho, Chiyoda-ku
Tokyo 102, Japan

0-324-01491-0

Library of Congress Cataloging-in-Publication Data

Terpstra, Vern
    International dimensions of marketing / Vern Terpstra, Lloyd C.
Russow. — 4th ed.
        p.   cm.
    Includes bibliographical references and index.
    ISBN 0-324-01491-0
    1. Export marketing. 2. Marketing.   I. Russow, Lloyd C.
II. Title.
HF1416.T47   1999
658.8′48—dc21

                                                                99-27837
                                                                CIP

To my wife, Bonnie

                              Vern Terpstra

To my parents, Erna and Erich

                              Lloyd Russow

P R E F A C E

I n order to study and understand the field of Marketing today, it is necessary to take into account its international ramifications. Even small
and medium-sized firms all over the world are posting web pages and
gaining access to customers in every continent. Communication is easier
and more widespread in developed and developing countries. Business
students need to be aware of these trends, and be prepared to use new
technologies in the marketing of ideas and products. The fourth edition of
International Dimensions of Marketing can be a helpful step in that
preparation. Previous editions of our text have been used at the under-
graduate level for basic marketing courses—which increasingly give emphasis to international issues—as well as at the graduate level in MBA
courses driven by cases and supplemented by readings.

Marketing now must encompass the needs and wants of a significantly
more diverse customer base. As we enter the new millennium, we discover
that global interdependence is here to stay. In the political realm, changes
in recent years have had global repercussions, including the fall of communism in eastern Europe, Hong Kong rule being passed back to China,
enlargement of NATO to include former enemies, India and Pakistan join-
ing the "nuclear club," the breakup of Czechoslovakia and Yugoslavia,

and the resumption of hostilities among Serbs, Croats, and Albanians. In the realm of economics, interdependence is clearly evident in the European Union as it undertakes monetary union and membership enlargement. Cooperation among NAFTA and MERCOSUR members is active in the Americas, and in ASEAN in the Far East. Capital and currency markets operate 24 hours a day. Countries are economically dependent on one another more than ever before as evident in ever-increasing trade and investment, as well as the reactions to recent financial crises in Asia and South America.

The fourth edition of ***International Dimensions of Marketing*** has built upon the success of our previous editions. We have added updated tables, examples, and recommended readings, new material on electronic data interchange, micro-marketing, integrated marketing communications, as well as discussions about the Internet as a resource for marketing research, distribution tool, and advertising medium. Also new to this edition is an index of web addresses for companies, organizations, and publications cited throughout the text. Because Internet addresses change, we recommend you refer to "Everything International," a set of web pages that serves as a gateway to a broad set of data, current event and news resources, and other items of interest to international marketers, whether practitioner, faculty, or student. The address is: *http://ib.philacol.edu/ib/russow.html*.

We thank the following reviewers for their time and suggestions:
Tevfik Dalgic
Utrecht Business School, The Netherlands

Clint B. Tankersly
Syracuse University

Joe K. Ballenger
Stephen F. Austin State University

Vern Terpstra
Lloyd Russow

ABOUT THE AUTHOR

V ern Terpstra is Professor Emeritus of International Business at the University of Michigan. He has authored twelve books and numerous articles that have appeared in U.S., European, and Asian journals. He is past president of the Academy of International Business and has been elected a Fellow of the Academy. He has taught at the Wharton School as well as in Britain, the Netherlands, China, Indonesia, Taiwan, and Zaire. He has consulted on international business issues with corporations in the United States and abroad, the U.S. government, the World Bank, and universities.

Lloyd Russow is the Coordinator of International Business Programs and Faculty at Philadelphia College of Textiles & Science (PCT&S). He has been teaching courses in international business, international marketing, trading blocs, and principles of marketing since he joined PCT&S in 1992. Lloyd has articles published in *Journal of Global Marketing, International Marketing Review, Journal of Studies in International Education,* and other journals. He is chair of the Academy of International Business, NE Chapter.

CONTENTS

C H A P T E R 1
Marketing and International Marketing

Why study international marketing? Such an exercise can only be justified if international marketing requires different knowledge and/or a distinctive competence. First let us consider the nature of marketing. Several common elements thread their way through the various definitions of marketing. *Marketing,* defined as the activities which connect a firm to its market and determine profitability, includes the following elements:

1. Analysis of the market
2. Development of products or services
3. Pricing of these products or services
4. Distribution—making the product or service available to the market
5. Promotion—informing and persuading the market

Marketing management involves the organization, planning, and control of all these activities.

What, then, is international marketing? In what way does marketing change when entering the international arena? We must recognize first that international marketing is *marketing.* It involves the same collection of activities as does domestic marketing. What distinguishes international marketing is not

1

the activities or functions performed but *the way they are performed.* The parameters of the international marketing task are different from those that influence domestic marketing. These influences will be described in detail as we discuss the various marketing functions in later chapters.

International marketing is, by definition, the act of marketing across national boundaries. The distinctiveness of the international marketing task comes from its three dimensions: (1) international marketing, (2) foreign marketing, and (3) multinational marketing.

1. The international marketing dimension involves *marketing across national borders.* Crossing a border confronts the marketer with new economic, political, and legal constraints, such as floating exchange rates, boycotts, and international law. These constraints usually force modification of the firm's marketing program as it crosses national boundaries.
2. The foreign marketing dimension concerns *marketing within foreign countries,* as when a U.S. firm markets in Belgium or Brazil. Such marketing is unlike domestic marketing because the firm faces different kinds of competition, consumer behavior, distribution channels, and promotional possibilities in Belgium or Brazil than it faces at home. The task is further complicated because each country has an individual, idiosyncratic marketing environment. In other words, Belgium is not only different from the United States; it is also different from Brazil or France, Iran or India. Thus, each foreign market presents a new challenge to the international marketer.
3. The multinational marketing dimension emphasizes the *coordination and integration* of the firm's marketing in diverse foreign environments. The unique nature of each foreign market fragments the international marketing effort and brings diseconomies of scale. The international marketer must carefully plan in order to maximize integration and synergy in the global marketing program while minimizing the costs of adapting to each foreign market.

THE NEED TO THINK INTERNATIONAL

Today more than ever, no country can isolate itself from the rest of the world. Terms such as *world economy, global village,* and *spaceship earth* indicate the interdependence facing all of us on this planet. For example, the ozone layer and global warming affect all countries; the Olympics represent a shared global experience; phenomena such as a rising or falling dollar, the price of oil, and nuclear proliferation are international rather than just national concerns. This interdependence of nations, however, is not the major reason why U.S. firms should think international. Their needs lie in more personal and selfish considerations.

U.S. firms find incentive to learn international marketing for two primary reasons: competition and markets. The *competition* facing them domestically is increasing from foreign firms, rather than just domestic companies. The problem is not just that Sony and Toyota are household names. Competition can be found in ham and golf carts from Poland and in shoes, clothing, cars, and cameras from such countries as Malaysia, Mexico, India, and China. In other words, competition comes not only from rich industrial nations, but also from Central Europe and developing nations. Like it or not, U.S. firms find themselves in a global marketplace where they must include global competitors in their competitive analysis.

The other major reason for U.S. firms to think international is to find *market opportunities* and growth. Markets mean people, and 95 percent of the world's population lives outside the United States. Of course, not all of those people can match the purchasing power of the U.S. citizen. Nevertheless, more than 75 percent of the world's purchasing power is found outside the United States. Therefore, the potential markets for many products and services are found abroad. To reach these markets, the firm must think international, as noted in Box 1-1.

BOX 1-1   *Exporting Pays Off*

Crystal International Corporation makes Crystal Hot Sauce. The firm originally began as a canning company of southern vegetables such as okra and yams in 1923. Crystal started exporting in 1959, shipping 1,200 cases of hot sauce to Saudi Arabia. Today, Crystal ships more than two million cases each year to 87 countries around the world.

Crystal products are manufactured at its plant in New Orleans, which has more than 275 employees. Exports constitute about 35 percent of Crystal's business, but Vice-President Marwan Kabbani sees growth opportunities in three areas:

1. Greater penetration in present markets, through increased advertising
2. Adding new products to the line
3. Reaching new markets, specifically Europe and Asia

(continued)

BOX 1-1   *Continued*

Crystal has worked regularly with the Department of Commerce district office in New Orleans for export information and assistance. "We have participated in a number of overseas trips organized by the Department's Gold Key Service and have received numerous leads as a result," notes Kabbani. Gold Key Service is a custom-tailored service for members of U.S. firms planning to visit a foreign country. It includes market research, orientation briefings, introduction to potential partners, and interpreters.

Source: *Business America*, January 1996, p. 18; M. M. Kabbani (personal communication, March 29, 1999)

To this point, our discussion has focused on the need for U.S. firms to think international. It is obvious, however, that the same arguments would generally apply to firms in other countries. In terms of market opportunities, European, Latin American, or Asian firms will have a smaller domestic market than do U.S. firms and, therefore, relatively greater opportunities in international marketing. Furthermore, they will usually be subject to the same kind of international competition that U.S. firms face. Europeans, for example, are as worried about Japanese competition as Americans are.

THE EXTENT OF INTERNATIONAL BUSINESS IN U.S. FIRMS

The largest U.S. firms have discovered the world market. Most *Fortune* 500 companies market internationally. The same is true of the larger accounting firms, advertising agencies, banks, and consulting firms. It should be noted that although our discussion and examples will often relate to manufacturing firms, international marketing is also necessary for service organizations, such as banks or accounting firms, as well as for public organizations such as the World Bank or the U.S. State Department. For example, for the five largest U.S. banks, foreign deposits average greater than 50 percent of the total. A dramatic indicator of U.S. international business involvement is the source of corporate profits, of which about one-third is from abroad. Furthermore, sales of U.S.–affiliated firms abroad are well over $1 trillion, a sum larger than the gross national product of most countries of the world. Exhibit 1-1 shows the extent of international involvement for selected U.S. companies.

EXHIBIT 1-1   *International Involvement of Selected U.S. Firms, 1997*

Company	Percent of Sales Abroad	Percent of Assets Abroad
Exxon	76	57
Manpower	73	74
Colgate-Palmolive	71	60
Mobil	68	61
Texas Instruments	67	37
Avon	65	59
Digital Equipment	64	45
Gillette	63	62
CPC International	61	62
McDonald's	60	55
Eastman Kodak	57	49
Int'l. Business Machines	57	49
Citicorp	55	63
Hewlett-Packard	54	54
Warner Lambert	53	53
Unisys	53	23
Minnesota Mining & Mfg.	52	39
Procter & Gamble	49	39
Dow Chemical	48	60
Xerox	48	55
Johnson & Johnson	48	49
Intel	45	16
General Electric	31	32
Merck	26	18
Disney	21	5

Source: Company annual reports.

International marketing is not an arena exclusively for large corporations however. More information is known about them because they are publicly owned and receive lots of publicity. Actually, thousands of small U.S. companies are engaged in international marketing. Indeed, 60 percent of U.S. exporters have fewer than 100 employees. These companies' names are not household words, but foreign markets are often as important to them as to many of the *Fortune* 500 firms. U.S. farmers, for example, are dependent on foreign markets. A different example of international marketing is the Pentagon, which does billions of dollars in business abroad. Actually, the Pentagon promotes the foreign sales of its domestic suppliers to reduce the cost of developing military hardware for the United States.

Although we have noted the extensive involvement of U.S. firms in international marketing, we do not deny that the majority of U.S. firms are not engaged in international marketing. Most of the small and medium-sized businesses in the United States are not selling abroad, but many more of them could be.

The Multinational Firm

We shall use the terms *international firm* and *multinational firm* somewhat interchangeably, or even just *multinational*. This term is used to designate a company that has production facilities in foreign countries. Multinationals obviously engage in international marketing, but a firm does not have to be a multinational to do so. Most U.S. firms selling abroad do not have foreign production facilities and thus can't be called multinationals. They have all of their production facilities in the United States, but some of them export to as many as 100 countries and are thus heavily engaged in international marketing. As we shall see, both multinationals and exporters are international marketers, but they face somewhat different marketing problems and opportunities.

ALTERNATIVE WAYS OF MARKETING INTERNATIONALLY

In 1997 world trade exceeded US $13 trillion ($6.8 trillion in imports and $6.6 trillion in exports, of which $4.9 trillion was accounted for by merchandise, $1.2 trillion in commercial services exports).[1] This immense volume of business was transacted in many different ways. Here we shall introduce some of the major methods firms use to sell to foreign markets. These methods of marketing internationally will be discussed in detail when we look at International Distribution Decisions.

Indirect Exporting

It is possible for the firm to sell its products abroad with minimal effort on its part when the sale is in fact a domestic sale. Several kinds of firms buy products in the United States and carry them to foreign markets.

---

[1]World Trade Organization <http://www.wto.org/wto/intltrad/internat.html>

- Multinational firms often incorporate U.S. equipment in their foreign factories. Many suppliers to multinationals began their international marketing in this way.
- Large foreign firms in manufacturing, mining, and retailing maintain procurement offices in the United States. They, too, have introduced many U.S. firms to foreign markets.
- International trading companies, most famous of which are the Japanese, also seek out U.S. goods they can sell in other markets.
- Export management companies, as their name implies, will take over the complete management of exports for a firm. They effectively act as the firm's export department even though they are a separate company. They are pure international marketing companies and service thousands of U.S. producers.

Direct Exporting

Direct export is the most common form of international marketing. In this form of entry, the firm takes responsibility for selling its products abroad. In this case the exporter or international marketer is based in the firm's domestic facilities and sells through distributors or agents in foreign markets.

Licensing

Licensing is international marketing by proxy. In a licensing arrangement, a domestic firm, the licensor, gives a foreign firm the right to produce and market its products in the licensee's country. In return, the licensor receives a royalty on sales. This practice allows, for example, a U.S. firm facing high transportation costs or duties in a foreign market to both produce and market its products there with no capital outlay and little effort on its part. It involves little international marketing effort and the product doesn't cross national borders because the licensee does the marketing in the foreign country.

Foreign Marketing Subsidiary

A firm's own sales/marketing office in a foreign country is called a marketing subsidiary. Firms operate foreign marketing subsidiaries for the same reasons they have their own salesforce domestically: more aggressive marketing and greater market share typically result when their own people rather than independent intermediaries are doing the marketing.

A foreign marketing subsidiary represents a much greater commitment by the firm than any of the methods discussed previously. It requires more money, personnel, and effort. The firm must not only market across national borders as it exports to its subsidiary, but also be responsible for marketing within the foreign country (foreign marketing). The increased profit potential often offsets the costs of the larger commitment.

Foreign Production by the Firm

The greatest commitment a firm can make to a foreign market is to have its own production facilities there. Foreign production usually costs much more money and causes more complications than any other method. It does not, however, mean a great difference in the international marketing process because most of the extra costs and problems are production-related rather than marketing-related. The international marketing task here remains essentially the same as with the foreign marketing subsidiary.

Many methods can be used to reach foreign markets, and we have noted just some of the major alternatives. These alternatives are available not only to U.S. firms but to any country's firms that wish to market internationally. Each method has its own constraints and opportunities. The marketing implications of these alternatives will be discussed in Chapters 4, 5, 6, 7, and 8.

INTERNATIONAL MARKETING: WHEN IN ROME, BE DIFFERENT

U.S. firms have been criticized for bringing their products and marketing methods into countries that are dissimilar to the United States. This action is sometimes called cultural imperialism. Several reasons explain why firms might try to market in foreign countries as they do at home.

1. The methods are proven in the sense that they probably made the firm successful in its home market.
2. The methods are what the firm knows best and thus represent the easiest and cheapest approach.
3. The firm can realize certain economies from a marketing program that is the same in all countries.

This standardized approach runs counter to the old advice: when in Rome, do as the Romans do. Although it may sound like reasonable counsel, competitive situations present two main reasons to question it. First, if one behaves like Romans while in their city, the Romans will probably win every time because they are very good at being Romans. Second, Rome has a lot of Romans and probably doesn't need any pseudo-Romans who probably won't contribute much to Rome, except more congestion. On the other hand, a foreigner with unique characteristics might be valued by the Romans for a variety of reasons.

The question of how to market in foreign countries has both public relations and economic aspects. That is, marketing relates to the firm's image as well as to its efficiency. The firm must ask itself, What is the most profitable way for us to market in foreign countries? Do we go native or do as we do at home? The firm will find no simple answer to that question. Indeed, in one way or another we will be addressing that issue throughout the rest of this book. An initial answer might be that the firm should do some of both: go native and do as it does at home. Finding the right balance between standardization and localization of marketing practices is one of the major challenges facing the international marketer. It faces McDonald's in Paris and Perrier and Toyota in Los Angeles. As a preliminary contribution to the discussion, Exhibit 1-2 presents some of the barriers to a completely standardized approach to marketing in foreign countries. The horizontal axis lists elements of a marketing program while the vertical axis shows some of the environmental factors that constrain a marketing program.

EXHIBIT 1-2   *Some Barriers to Standardized International Marketing*

Obstacles to Uniformity	Marketing Ingredients			
	Product	Price	Distribution	Promotion
Economic Factors	Varied income levels	Varied income levels	Different retail structures	Media availability
Cultural Factors	Consumer tastes and habits	Price negotiating habits	Shopping habits	Language and attitude differences
Competitive Factors	Nature of existing products	Competitors' costs and prices	Competitors' monopoly of channels	Competitors' budget and appeal
Legal Factors	Product regulations	Price controls	Restrictions on distribution	Advertising and media restrictions

COMPANY INFLUENCES ON INTERNATIONAL MARKETING

The nature of the job facing the international marketer can vary on several dimensions. One is the level of the firm's involvement or method of entry into the foreign market. For example, working with a licensee is quite different from working with a marketing subsidiary. Another set of influences comes from the environment in which the marketer operates, as well as the foreign economies and their cultures. Some of these elements are indicated in Exhibit 1-2 and will be discussed further in Chapter 2. A third set of influences arises from within the company itself, requiring a case approach to determining strategy. Here we look at the major company characteristics that influence international marketing.

Company Size and Resources

A *Fortune* 500 company that decides to go international obviously has more strategic alternatives than does the small firm making the same decision. The large firm typically has more resources to be able to enter more countries with a wider product line and a more direct entry method, that is, foreign production or marketing subsidiaries. The international marketer in such a firm has a different task from the small firm's marketer who must begin with a smaller number of markets and a lesser involvement, such as independent distributors or licensees. International marketing for Coca-Cola is quite a different challenge from international marketing for Dr. Pepper, for example.

Role of Top Management

When the business press (*Business Week, Forbes, Fortune, The Wall Street Journal,* etc.) profiles a U.S. company, it often stresses the role of the executive in the success of the firm. Generally speaking, top management significantly affects the direction and fortunes of a company. That notion holds true for international marketing as well. Various studies of a firm's international involvement have shown that the chief executive is the critical factor in whether a firm goes international and how it goes international.

- Kellogg has been an international business almost from the beginning. W. K. Kellogg opened a plant in Canada in 1914. Succeeding presidents continued this expansion until more than 40 percent of Kellogg's sales came from abroad by 1997. Chairman Arnold Langbo said however, "The exciting issue for the '90s is geographic expansion." One goal, included in their 1997 management philosophy, is to "strengthen our global leadership in ready-to-eat cereal."

- The chairman and CEO of Procter & Gamble and formerly the head of P&G International, John Pepper doubled foreign sales and profits in just three years. With sales over $3.5 billion in 1997, 49 percent of sales and 37 percent of profits were generated outside the United States. This growth represented gains in established markets as well as entry into Central Europe, Russia, China, and India.
- Perrier was number two in the French beverage market behind Evian. The president of Perrier, however, was an internationally oriented person and led Perrier to a significant position in foreign markets. This direction contrasted with Evian management's approach, which was originally to remain essentially a domestic company in France.

Company History and Experience

Each firm is blessed or cursed with a unique history. The background places it in a particular situation with different strategic alternatives, both domestically and internationally. For this reason international marketing is a somewhat different task in each company.

- Coca-Cola was first and largest of the overseas soft drink marketers. Its strong position abroad made Pepsi-Cola's international marketing both difficult and different. Coke successfully pioneered cola drinks in foreign markets and obtained high market share and a position of price leadership. Coming into these markets later, Pepsi faced a difficult competitive challenge rather than a pioneering marketing task.
- In the United States, Campbell Soup and H. J. Heinz compete in several product categories. Though the two firms are about the same size, Campbell's has been much bigger in the United States. Competitive positions are reversed overseas where Heinz has been longer established and much bigger. As a newer, smaller entrant to foreign markets, Campbell's faces a different international marketing task from that of Heinz.

Organization for International Business

An international marketer's job responsibilities will vary according to the way the firm organizes for worldwide business. For example, where the firm has an international division for its business abroad, the marketing manager may have responsibility for all products in all foreign markets, a large task indeed. Where the firm has product divisions with global responsibilities, the product or brand manager would be responsible for all countries, but for a limited number of products. Where the firm has an area structure with divisions for Europe, Latin America, and so on, the marketer may be in charge of all of the firm's products but with market responsibility for only a part of the world, say, Latin America.

Product and Industry

The distinction between industrial and consumer marketing is as valid internationally as domestically. The international marketer faces a different task in General Foods than in General Motors, a different job in Upjohn than in Union Carbide, and still different in Chase Manhattan than in Colgate-Palmolive. Because customers' needs and buying behavior vary according to the product or service involved, so does the marketer's task of satisfying the customer, at home or abroad.

SUMMARY

This chapter has introduced the nature of international marketing management and presented similarities as well as differences between domestic and international marketing. These are topics that will be expanded on in succeeding chapters. Before continuing with that discussion, however, we must take some time to consider a matter as important to the task as a passport is to international travel; that is, the environment in which the international marketer operates, the subject of Chapter 2.

QUESTIONS

1. How does international marketing differ from domestic marketing?
2. Distinguish between international marketing, foreign marketing, and multinational marketing.
3. Why should firms consider markets outside their home country?
4. Identify and discuss the different ways firms can reach foreign markets.
5. Why do firms like to market abroad the same way they do at home? What hinders them from doing so?
6. Show how company characteristics can affect the nature of the international marketing task.

FURTHER READING

1. Bartels, Robert, "Are Domestic and International Marketing Dissimilar?" *Journal of Marketing* (July 1968), pp. 56–61.
2. Cateora, Philip R. and John L. Graham, *International Marketing,* 10th ed. (Boston, MA: Irwin/McGraw-Hill, 1999), Chapter 1.
3. Jain, Subhash C., *International Marketing Management,* 5th ed. (Cincinnati, OH: South-Western College Publishing, 1996), Chapter 1.
4. Levitt, Theodore, "Globalization of Markets," *Harvard Business Review* (May-June 1983), pp. 92–102.
5. Terpstra, Vern, and Ravi Sarathy, *International Marketing,* 7th ed. (Fort Worth, TX: Dryden Press, 1997), Chapters 1 and 6.

NOTE: Basic marketing texts usually discuss the definition and nature of marketing in the first chapter.

C H A P T E R   2

The Environment of International Marketing

arketing is not only an economic activity but a social activity as well. As such, the way it is conducted will depend on the human environment or culture in which it takes place. Basic U.S. marketing texts usually have one or more chapters that discuss the environment and its impact on marketing programs. Marketing is, after all, a kind of adaptive behavior by the firm, and marketing managers must become acquainted with the elements to which they must adapt. The environment of international marketing is obviously more complex than the task facing a domestic marketer in any one country. Rather than attempting to cover that environment extensively, which would require a volume to itself, we will identify the critical dimensions of that environment and provide the marketing manager with an idea of what to look for.

RELATIONSHIP MARKETING

The environment in which international marketers operate highlights the importance of *relationship marketing*. Relationships between the firm and its customers, suppliers, distributors, and others with whom the company

BOX 2-1 *The Dynamic World Economy*

HEADLINES OF 1997 INDICATING THE VOLATILITY OF THE GLOBAL ENVIRONMENT

- The *Nakhodka*, a Russian-owned tanker carrying 119,000 barrels of oil, breaks in two off the coast of Japan.
- Madeleine Albright is sworn in as U.S. Secretary of State, the first woman to hold the job.
- Cyberjaya, an "intelligent" city, is established in Malaysia.
- Princess Diana, Mother Teresa, Giann Versace, and former Crown Prince Haile Selassie die.
- Mergers and acquisitions include the Union Bank of Switzerland and Swiss Bank Group union to become largest bank in Europe (assets: $625 billion), Boeing's acquisition of McDonnell Douglas ($16.5 billion), WorldCom besting of British Telecommunications in MCI acquisition ($42.6 billion).
- In partial settlement of an industrial espionage suit, Volkswagen acknowledged the "possibility of illegal activities" and agreed to pay $100 million to General Motors.
- Ethnic unrest continues in Burundi; Tutsi-dominated army kills 126 Hutu refugees returning from Tanzania.
- Hurricane Pauline makes landfall near Acapulco, Mexico, killing at least 50 people.
- Myanmar joins the Association of Southeast Asian Nations (ASEAN).
- Currency crisis hits Asia.
- Intel CEO Andy Grove is Time's "Man of the Year."
- The Casablanca Stock Exchange is initiated.
- South Koreans elect Kim Dae Jung president.
- U.S. common stock issuance totals $120 billion, bonds issued exceed $1 trillion, and mergers and acquisitions top $650 billion.
- Coup in Cambodia.
- Internet becomes available in Ethiopia.
- Famine in North Korea, thousands suspected dead.
- U.S. stock market declines over 500 points in one day, but ends year up by 21 percent. Markets elsewhere (East versus West): Nikkei (Tokyo) and Hang Seng (Hong Kong) down more than 25 percent for the year; IPC (Mexico City) and DAX (Germany) up more than 25 percent; FT-SE 100 (London) up 20 percent.

wishes to maintain long-term relationships are recognized as a significant aspect of enduring success. In the United States, business people tend to focus on short-term profit and return to shareholders, primarily because stockholders would divest themselves of the stock if the firm didn't. This focus presents a dilemma for the global firm however. If much of the capital comes from equity and the investors are short-term oriented, the firm is at a disadvantage relative to the firm that gets much of its capital from debt instruments and investors who tend to be more long-term oriented.

International marketers are well aware that they cannot use foreign markets as dumping grounds for excess capacity, only to discontinue supply to their customers when the home market is good. For example, a common complaint among Europeans in the 1970s and 1980s was that U.S. companies were not dependable and were liable to ignore foreign sales when the U.S. market rebounded. A company and its people must be committed to its international markets.

Another important relationship is the one firms have with employees. In the United States, it is not uncommon to fire salespeople who are not meeting expectations. In other countries, the relationship between a firm and its representatives may not be easy or cheap to dissolve.

Perhaps, because of the inherent foreignness of the international environment, the importance of establishing and maintaining ties between the company and its various stakeholders (customers, suppliers, employees, and investors) has been recognized among international marketers for some time.

INTERNATIONAL ENVIRONMENT

The environment of international marketing has two major aspects, the international environment and the domestic environment in foreign markets. We begin by looking at the international environment. As Exhibit 2-1 shows, when the firm sells abroad from its domestic plants, the products pass through an international environment (a sort of checkpoint) before entering foreign markets. As they pass through this environment, various international economic and political forces may hinder the firm's international marketing. In this section we will discuss the most important of these international economic and political forces.

A tourist traveling from one country to another faces certain economic, political, and legal constraints not encountered in domestic travel. The

EXHIBIT 2-1   *The International Environment of International Marketing*

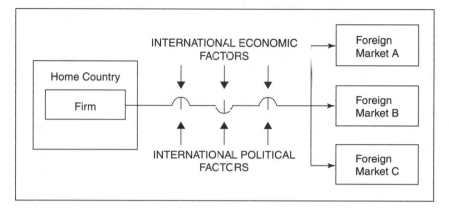

same factors affect the international movement of goods. When we speak of international marketing, we emphasize the role of the firm in moving its goods or services between nations. When a firm sells across national boundaries, it is engaging in international trade as well as international marketing. Because this kind of marketing is not possible without international trade, the international marketer needs an understanding of the whys and hows of international trade.

WHY INTERNATIONAL TRADE?

The volume of international trade is an indicator of the economic interdependence of nations. Perhaps the most striking economic development since World War II is the growth of world trade. Such trade has grown an average of about 7 percent each year, reaching $13 trillion by 1997. By contrast, world gross national product has grown at only about half that rate. This difference means that the share of international trade in world economic activity has more than doubled since 1945 and that nations are more interdependent than ever before. For firms it means growing access to the markets of the world and growing competition at home.

Understanding why nations trade is essential to international marketing planning. A look at the different kinds of trading nations can help us understand this issue. Before World War II, when many countries were colonies, their trade and economic activities were directed by an absent

colonial power. Today almost all of these countries are independent politically, but their international trade is bigger than ever. Communist ideol-
ogy supports *autarky,* or economic self-sufficiency, yet we see the former
communist countries now expanding their trade. Even China has joined
the game. The industrialized market economies of western Europe, North
America, and Japan are the biggest traders of all, accounting for about
two-thirds of all world trade. Thus we see nations with differing levels of
economic development, political ideologies, and economic structures all
engaging in international trade. What is the attraction of this trade that it
can surmount such great economic and political differences?

Nations trade with other nations because they find they are better off
by trading than by going it alone. The reason relates to Adam Smith's famous finding about the source of the wealth of nations. Smith said nations
become wealthy when they practice specialization and the division of labor. Each person or economic unit that specializes in what it does best creates a greater output for all to share (the nation's wealth). When nations
specialize in what they do best and trade this output for what other nations
do best, each party is better off. Economists call it the Principle of Comparative Advantage. This principle states that because nations are en-
dowed with differing amounts and kinds of human and natural resources,
they have differing abilities to produce varied goods and services, making
trade both possible and desirable.

Will Trade Continue?

Because international trade offers benefits to each trading nation, it has
grown dramatically in absolute and relative terms, especially since World
War II. *International trade permits firms to market their goods across national borders.* The international marketing planner is concerned, therefore, about the future of international trade. Let us look at some of the
major variables the marketer must consider in predicting the future course
of world trade.

Population and Income Growth

Growth in the world's population and especially in the world's income is
favorable to trade. Consumption is a function of income and, significantly,
the purchase of foreign goods rises relatively more with increased income
than does the purchase of domestic goods. In almost every country, im-

ported goods have a higher *income elasticity* than domestic goods, to use the economist's term. Income elasticity refers to the relationship between a change in income and a corresponding change in demand. If elasticity is high and income rises, demand also rises, but at a faster rate. This explains why world trade has grown twice as fast as world income since World War II.

Comparative Advantage

Most nations cannot supply all of their needs from domestic resources. They find it to their advantage to specialize in the things they are relatively efficient at producing and to trade for things that other nations are relatively efficient in supplying. As long as nations differ in their human and natural resources endowment, and thus their economic capabilities, they will be motivated to engage in international specialization and trade.

War and Peace

Trade is a peaceful, though sometimes political, form of international relations. Part of the reason for the great increase in world trade since 1945 is that, relatively speaking, the world has been at peace. Any increase in international tension—cold war or open conflict—reduces international trade and marketing. Boycotts and embargoes become the rule; no trading with the enemy. In 1994, the United States lifted its 19-year trade embargo on Vietnam, but then it passed the Burton-Helms Act of 1996 to further restrict trade with Cuba.

Technological Change

Recent decades have seen major improvements in transportation, storage, and communications capabilities in the form of cargo jets, supertankers, containerized shipping, FastShips, computers, and satellites. Technological advances have afforded firms the ability to provide better services for the customers and meet individual needs better (made-to-measure clothes and bicycles, for instance). Electronic data interchange means that firms can respond to intermediaries' needs more quickly, which in turn can lead to more efficient inventory, stocking, and shipping strategies. Global positioning systems (GPS) allows for better tracking and transporting of merchandise.

The contribution of communication advances, on the other hand, has been an improvement in information systems of both producer and consumer, expanding the market. Cellular telephones and computers are examples of communication developments that have expanded markets in the United States and worldwide.

The Internet provides firms with a broader audience. Products can be promoted and sold via the personal computer worldwide; as computers continue to go down in price, more people will be included in this audience. This trend is a double-edged sword. It also means that small and medium-sized firms can enter the global arena more easily and quicker than before leading to increased competition. It also means that consumers will come to the marketplace better informed and able to compare alternatives more easily.

Improvements in the movement of goods and people include the Eurostar train between the United Kingdom and continental Europe (the "chunnel") and the FastShip, which will be able to carry 10,000 tons and cross the Atlantic in just four days. Cheaper transportation means that more goods can be shipped abroad. As an extreme case consider the days of Columbus when ocean shipping was so expensive that only spices and precious metals could pay the freight. Most goods consumed then were domestic goods in contrast to today when most nations have a large import content in their consumption.

Advances in many areas continue to improve the processes with which things are made, as well as the products and services. Whether referring to new medical diagnostic capabilities, scanning and tracking devices for packages, or longer-lasting automobiles and more powerful computers, technological advances have far-reaching effects on businesses, whether the firm is domestic or international.

International Monetary System

Marketers are involved in an exchange of goods or services for money. Money is the medium of exchange, which is generally true in international trade as well as domestic trade, except for some barter transactions. However, a nation can't buy foreign goods with its domestic money. It must have internationally acceptable money, usually gold or a hard currency in which traders have confidence. Currently, U.S. dollars are by far the most widely used medium of exchange in international trade, followed by the deutsche mark, the pound sterling, and the yen. By the end of 2002, the

Euro will replace many of the European currencies, and some speculation has the Euro supplanting the U.S. dollar as the world's major currency.

If a nation doesn't have gold mines, the primary way it can acquire foreign money is by selling its goods abroad. *The international marketing firm has a vital interest in the financial situation of the world's markets. The firm cannot export into those countries that do not have internationally traded money.*

A country has no international financial problems as long as it can sell enough abroad to pay for what it wants to buy from other countries. Unfortunately, many nations have international trade deficits; they buy more from others than they sell abroad. Countries that continue to incur international deficits soon exhaust their reserves of international money. They then have to cut back their international trade and lose its benefits unless they can find a friend to help them, or unless the international monetary system can help by extending credit to them. Some understanding of this system is necessary if one is to evaluate the future of international trade.

During the Great Depression of the 1930s, each country tried to salvage its own economy. Nationalistic actions were taken, often at the expense of others. They were called "beggar-my-neighbor" policies, such as using tariffs or quotas to keep out foreign goods in an effort to maintain domestic employment. These policies were doubly unfortunate. First, they hurt foreign countries by stopping their exports and hindering their recovery. Second, they did nothing to help the countries that practiced them because their employment and exports did not increase either. Because of this bad experience, a number of countries gathered at Bretton Woods, New Hampshire, at the close of World War II to avoid a repetition of this economic disaster. One of the results of that meeting was the creation of the International Monetary Fund (IMF).

The IMF became an organization to promote international financial cooperation and to supply international liquidity by loans to member countries. Most countries have joined the IMF, including many of the former communist countries. The IMF has been a contributing factor in the dynamic growth of international trade since World War II. Its contributions have been twofold. First, by setting rules of behavior and promoting cooperation among members, it has greatly diminished the amount of nationalistic behavior, thus removing financial barriers to international trade. Second, the IMF is also a fund, or pool, of international money, partly in gold with the rest in the currencies of member countries. The IMF uses this pool of reserves to lend to members facing deficits in their international payments. This system allows the countries to continue trading until they can correct their payments problems. The IMF has undergone certain changes in recent years, but as long as it can continue to promote international monetary cooperation and lend reserves to deficit countries, the picture for world trade is more encouraging. Continued IMF success will also mean more open world markets for international marketers.

WTO-GATT versus Protectionism

International trade fell to a low ebb in the 1930s not only because countries imposed payments restrictions, as already noted, but also because countries interfered with the physical movement of goods by placing tariffs and quotas on foreign goods. A *tariff* is a tax or duty on goods from another country. A *quota* is a specific restriction on the quantity of foreign goods entering a country, e.g., pairs of shoes or tons of steel. For example, under the Hawley-Smoot Act of 1930, the United States had many tariffs of as much as 100 percent of the value of the imported goods. How many imported Toyotas and Sonys would U.S. consumers buy if their price were doubled with such a tariff? Such actions of course invited retaliation by other countries, so eventually few goods were being sold internationally and the benefits of international trade were lost.

In the aftermath of World War II, an agreement was created to avoid a repetition of this unhappy experience—the General Agreement on Tariffs and Trade, or GATT. Whereas the IMF fought to eliminate restrictions on international payments, GATT fought restrictive commercial policies affecting the movement of goods. As we discussed, these restrictive, nationalistic policies hurt other nations. They are also called *protectionist* policies because their primary purpose is usually to protect domestic employment and industry. Demands for protection invariably arise from the workers and/or managers of an industry whose employment and sales have been reduced by competition from imports.

Up to the mid-1970s, GATT played a major role in reducing barriers to trade. U.S. tariffs, for example, dropped from an average level above 50 percent in the 1930s to an average level of less than 10 percent by 1980. GATT's activities in this area have been a major factor in the great expansion of international trade that has occurred during its existence. GATT has achieved this progress in two ways. One is by establishing a code of good behavior and a cooperative framework among its members. This approach is similar to what the IMF has done on the payments side.

GATT has also reduced the amount of beggar-my-neighbor policymaking. GATT is, in effect, the world trade club with more than 130 members and associates, roughly the same membership as the IMF. The members of these two groups account for the bulk of world trade, and therefore any progress they make expands the total volume of world trade.

The second means employed by GATT to expand trade has been periodic multilateral tariff negotiations. These multinational bargaining sessions are usually held in Geneva, where up to 100 nations get together to bargain down the barriers against each other's goods. During the 1950s and 1960s when the barriers were higher and the spirit of cooperation greater, significant reductions in trade barriers were achieved. In the 1970s only one negotiation was held, the Tokyo Round, which ran from 1974 to 1979. Although 99 countries participated for several years, rather small additional gains were made. The next round, the Uruguay Round, lasted from 1986 to 1994.

Even though GATT was successful in reducing tariff barriers worldwide, the increased use of nontariff barriers such as quotas and subsidies went largely ignored. Trade in services, such as banking and accounting, also increased since the late 1940s, and GATT unfortunately focused primarily on manufactured goods. Countries had also become concerned about the general lack of intellectual property protection and the lax enforcement of existing patent, trademark, and copyright laws. Using GATT as its foundation, the World Trade Organization (WTO) was created in 1995 in order to address these issues.

What will WTO's role be in the future? Hopefully, the organization will be around for some time, but there is less room for optimism about similar progress in the future. In the early years after World War II, nations were recovering from the effects of both the Great Depression and the war. The feeling of failure and the need for cooperation were strong enough so that collaborative organizations could be formed and real progress made. During the 1970s new problems arose: high oil prices and balance of payments deficits, inflation, and recession. As these problems persisted, countries began to worry more about saving their own economy and less about international cooperation. Hence, the Tokyo Round made only modest progress after five years of negotiation.

High unemployment in some parts of the world will mean continuing demands by workers for protection against imports. Also, increasing cooperation among regional groups of countries, such as the European Union, NAFTA, and MERCOSUR, puts regional concerns above the worldwide attempts to increase trade. Still, the international marketer would be likely to support WTO in its endeavors to moderate protectionist demands. After all, while imports may threaten employment, they also pay for the country's exports, which increase employment, generally in higher-wage industries. The international firm would naturally prefer to be able to export to world markets without facing protectionist restrictions.

INTERNATIONAL POLITICS

The typical firm considers itself primarily an economic rather than a political organization. When marketing internationally, however, a firm will often be affected by political issues, usually against its will. International politics is concerned with the relation between individual countries, say Vietnam and the United States, or between groups of countries, say EU and NAFTA, or North-South relations. International relations is a vast subject; here we shall identify certain aspects of it that affect international marketing.

Bilateral Relations

When a country trades with any other, the economic side of their relationship can't be considered in isolation from their overall relationship, which includes political, cultural, legal, and military aspects. For example, when Russia invaded Afghanistan, response from the United States came on several levels that included a cutback on trade and a boycott of the Moscow Olympics that year. This example serves as just one illustration of the fact that a firm cannot be a successful international marketer if it ignores these noneconomic parameters. The United States (or any other country) has a unique relationship with each country in the world. The quality of these relationships can either help or hinder a firm's international marketing efforts. Consider, for instance, the booming trade the United States enjoys with South Korea and Taiwan in contrast to its almost nonexistent trade with Iraq and Libya. These bilateral relationships need continuous monitoring because they evolve over time and may even change abruptly, as happened, for example, in our dealings with Russia before and after their invasion of Afghanistan, or with China before and after Tienanmen Square.

Some examples further illustrate the variety of bilateral relationships:

- Before 1960, U.S. companies targeted Cuba as a major international market. When Castro came to power, however, that business ceased immediately. A similar development occurred in Iran after Khomeini's rise to power.
- Israel's trading partners are determined more by politics than by economics to an extent greater than that of any other country in the world. Nations friendly to the Arab side of the conflict will not trade with Israel; Israel can only deal with nations that accept or support it politically.
- France dominates the external trade of several African nations. Colonial rule has been dissolved in these countries, but their French language and cultural ties continue to give French firms a competitive advantage there.

Multilateral Relations

Nations like to conduct independent foreign policy, but they frequently find it necessary or useful to act in concert with others. Military alliances are usually marriages of convenience or necessity, but so are most other international groupings. Each country in a group shares only partially in its aims and methods. Nevertheless, to the degree that they act together, they must be considered collectively. For example, OPEC is a group of petroleum exporting countries that has maintained sufficient unity to command attention as an organization of nations.

East-West

The most familiar example of collective international relations used to be the East-West split between communist nations and the West. Although it was essentially a political-military difference, it also had important economic implications. Trade was restricted between the two groups, especially in technical or military items. With the collapse of communism in the East, an economic and political rapprochement has taken place between the two sides. Trade and economic relations are likely to expand greatly as the central European countries adjust their political and economic systems to more democratic market economies.

North-South

Perhaps the most important division in the world economy is the one between rich and poor, developed and developing nations, the industrialized nations and the Third World, or simply North versus South. This division of the world became especially visible at a United Nations meeting in Geneva in 1964 where 123 nations gathered to consider the needs and demands of the developing countries. The designation of a North-South split is increasingly appropriate. The idea behind the geographic designation is that the critical problem is not communism versus capitalism or democracy, but the haves versus the have-nots. The terms *South* and *North* are appropriate because the Third World countries are all tropical or subtropical, whereas almost all industrialized countries are in the Northern Hemisphere. The North and South were clearly delineated at the Geneva meeting by the voting. The North voted "No" on most proposals, with the Soviet Union and the United States on the same side, while the South collectively voted "Yes."

Though the South obtained no immediate satisfaction at the Geneva meeting, it was the first step in an ongoing journey. To help the South in its move toward economic development, the United Nations Conference on Trade and Development (UNCTAD) was created. UNCTAD articulates the needs of developing countries. It directs the attention of nations of the North toward ways they can provide greater aid and help in trade. It encourages companies of the developed nations, through their trade and manufacturing activities, to play a greater role in the economic development of the South. UNCTAD has brought international business into international politics, which has of course greatly influenced many firms' international marketing programs.

Other organizations also affect international marketing, such as Food and Agricultural Organization (FAO), World Health Organization (WHO), the World Bank Group (IBRD), the International Telecommunications Union (ITU). Although space does not permit us to consider them all here, we have attempted with our discussion to alert the international marketer to the importance of international political considerations to the success of the firm's business abroad.

In looking at the international environment of international marketing, we noted some of the constraints and opportunities posed by developments in international economics and politics. We observed how major international organizations, such as the IMF, WTO-GATT, and UNCTAD can influence the environment and operations of international marketers. We now turn to the second part of the environment of international marketing, the domestic environment in the foreign markets of the firm.

FOREIGN MARKET ENVIRONMENT

The study of the international environment can often be overwhelming; however the marketer may feel somewhat more comfortable when looking at the situation within foreign markets. Though each foreign market is unique, the marketer at least can use the same checklist for analyzing foreign market environments that is used in the firm's domestic market. Just as the marketing variables (product, price, promotion, and distribution) are present in every country, so are the uncontrollable environmental factors that affect the marketing mix. Exhibit 2-2 illustrates the relationship that would apply in any country: the firm's marketing program (the inner circle) is constrained and shaped by the economy, the legal system, and the social and political forces of the surrounding host country.

EXHIBIT 2-2 *Marketing Mix and Environment*

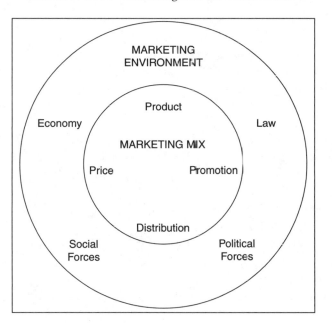

THE ECONOMY

Population

A firm's first concern in looking at a foreign country is the size of the market. Markets are people with money; therefore the study of market size begins by looking at population and income figures. Of the more than 200 political entities recognized by the United Nations, 150 have a population of one million or more. Generally, firms are most interested in these markets, though some products will find interesting markets in even smaller countries, such as Kuwait or the United Arab Emirates. To a U.S. firm, most foreign markets might seem small. However, about one-fourth of the world's nations have a population of 15 million or more—a market size of potential interest to all kinds of firms. These countries are shown in Exhibit 2-3. Even among these countries tremendous differences are evident.

In addition to the numbers, two other aspects of population deserve attention: the age distribution and the geographic distribution or density. Consumers have different needs and purchasing power over their life cycles. Therefore, the marketer must analyze the age distribution of a given population before estimating the market potential. Many developing countries, for example, have 40 percent or more of their population in the 0–14 age group, a group that is usually dependent and economically inactive. In western Europe, by contrast, only about 20 percent are in the 0–14 age group. In the over 65 age group, western Europe's percentage is more than three times that of the developing countries. Such variations suggest that two countries with similar population size may not only have different market potential, but also needs for different kinds of goods and services.

Population density has to do with the ease of *reaching* a market rather than the size of the market. When a market is more concentrated, the firm's logistics and communications are easier. On this basis, a country such as The Netherlands, with 1,200 persons per square mile, is more attractive than Norway, with about 36 persons per square mile. Because international marketers usually consider a number of markets rather than just one, they might look at population density for a region rather than for one country in isolation. The data then would show the attraction of western Europe, which has an average population density four times greater than that of South America and two times greater than Africa.

EXHIBIT 2-3   *Countries with a Population Greater Than 15 Million, 1996*

	Country	Population (millions)		Country	Population (millions)
1.	China	1,215	29.	South Africa	38
2.	India	945	30.	Colombia	37
3.	United States	265	31.	Argentina	35
4.	Indonesia	197	32.	Tanzania	30
5.	Brazil	161	33.	Canada	30
6.	Russian Federation	148	34.	Algeria	29
7.	Pakistan	134	35.	Kenya	27
8.	Japan	126	36.	Sudan	27
9.	Bangladesh	122	37.	Morocco	27
10.	Nigeria	115	38.	Peru	24
11.	Mexico	93	39.	Afghanistan	24
12.	Germany	82	40.	Uzbekistan	23
13.	Vietnam	75	41.	Romania	23
14.	Philippines	72	42.	Korea, Dem. Rep. (North)	22
15.	Turkey	63			
16.	Iran, Islamic Rep.	63	43.	Venezuela	22
17.	Thailand	60	44.	Nepal	22
18.	Egypt, Arab Rep.	59	45.	Iraq	21
19.	United Kingdom	59	46.	Malaysia	21
20.	France	58	47.	Uganda	20
21.	Ethiopia	58	48.	Saudi Arabia	19
22.	Italy	57	49.	Australia	18
23.	Ukraine	51	50.	Sri Lanka	18
24.	Myanmar	46	51.	Mozambique	18
25.	Korea, Rep. (South)	46	52.	Ghana	18
26.	Congo, Dem. Rep.	45	53.	Kazakstan	16
27.	Spain	39	54.	Yemen. Rep.	16
28.	Poland	39	55.	Netherlands	16

Source: The *World Development Indicators 1998 CD-ROM,* The International Bank for Reconstruction & Development/The World Bank.

Income

Two measures of income are needed to evaluate market potential: per capita income and total national income or gross national product (GNP). Each tells a different story about the market. Consumer goods marketers are especially interested in per capita income, which correlates with the purchasing behavior of consumers. Indeed, on an international level, income becomes an important variable in explaining the types of items consumers buy in different countries. Per capita incomes range from about $20,000 or more in such countries as Canada, Japan, Switzerland, and the United States, to less than $500 in some Asian and African nations. These tremendous differences in income are matched by equally varied market baskets of consumer goods. Exhibit 2-4 indicates the range of incomes within major regions of the world. Note the great spread between the highest per capita incomes and the smallest—a difference greater than one hundredfold.

We must note one caveat about per capita income figures. They are useful country descriptors to the extent that most of the people are near that average figure. Unfortunately, many countries have a bimodal distribution of income with a small part of the population getting incomes well above the national average and the majority of the people receiving incomes less than the average. In these countries with dual economies (one rich and one poor, with no middle class) the per capita figure can be misleading. For example, in India, about 80 million people have European-size incomes, whereas more than 700 million Indians are below the per capita figure stated for India. In such cases, the marketer must analyze each part of the economy separately rather than relying on the per capita figure.

Another consideration when comparing income is the relative purchasing power in each country. Purchasing Power Parity (PPP) is an economic theory linking inflation rates and currency exchange rates. Simply put, the theory states that inflation rate differences between two countries will be offset by equal, but opposite changes in the currency exchange rates between two (or more) countries in the long run. The argument supporting the PPP theory is that if differences in real prices do exist, people would engage in arbitrage (simultaneously buying in the market where the good is cheap, thereby driving up the price, and selling it in the country where the good is expensive, making it more plentiful and driving the price down) until the prices where equal. By adjusting the GNP per capita figures in Exhibit 2-4, the income averages reflect consumers' real buying power and are more meaningful than simple GNP per capita figures.

A second measure of income indicative of market size is gross domestic product (GDP). It is a more reliable indicator of the potential for industrial goods. Exhibit 2-5 lists the countries with a GDP of $70 billion or more. It is instructive to compare and contrast the countries in Exhibit 2-5 with those in Exhibit 2-3, which have 15 million or more population. Population and GDP don't correlate very well.

EXHIBIT 2-4 *Per Capita Income of Major Regions and Selected Countries, 1996*

Region and Country	GNP per Capita (US S)	GNP per Capita, PFP (US $)
North America		
Canada	19,020	21,380
Mexico	3,670	7,660
United States	28,020	28,020
Western Europe		
France	26,270	21,510
Greece	11,460	12,730
Switzerland	44,350	26,340
United Kingdom	19,600	19,960
Latin America		
Argentina	8,380	9,530
Bolivia	830	2,860
Brazil	4,400	6,340
Chile	4,860	11,700
Africa		
Cameroon	610	1,760
Ghana	360	1,790
Nigeria	240	870
South Africa	3,520	7,450
Asia		
China	750	3,330
India	380	1,580
Japan	40,940	23,420
Korea, Rep. (South)	10,610	13,080

Source: *The World Development Indicators, 1998 CD-ROM*, The International Bank for Reconstruction & Development/The World Bank.

Let us note some uses and limitations of our two income figures as market indicators. Using per capita income figures, a country such as South Korea looks much more attractive than China, because Korea's figure is over $10,000, or nearly 15 times as large as China's. However, China's total GDP is about one-and-half times as large as South Korea's because its population is 25 times larger.

Another comparison would be Switzerland and India. Switzerland's per capita income, adjusted for purchasing power is over $26,000, or 17 times

EXHIBIT 2-5   *World's Largest Economies, 1996*

Rank	Country	GDP ($billions)	Rank	Country	GDP ($billions)
1.	United States	$7,342	20.	Sweden	250
2.	Japan	4,600	21.	Austria	226
3.	Germany	2,353	22.	Indonesia	226
4.	France	1,540	23.	Thailand	185
5.	Italy	1,208	24.	Turkey	181
6.	United Kingdom	1,146	25.	Denmark	174
7.	China	815	26.	Norway	158
8.	Brazil	749	27.	Hong Kong, China	155
9.	Spain	582	28.	Poland	134
10.	Canada	579	29.	South Africa	126
11.	Korea, Rep. (South)	485	30.	Finland	124
12.	Russian Federation	441	31.	Greece	123
13.	Australia	393	32.	Portugal	104
14.	Netherlands	392	33.	Malaysia	99
15.	India	356	34.	Singapore	94
16.	Mexico	335	35.	Colombia	85
17.	Argentina	295	36.	Philippines	84
18.	Switzerland	293	37.	Chile	74
19.	Belgium	264	38.	Ireland	70

Source: *The World Development Indicators, 1998 CD-ROM*, The International Bank for Reconstruction & Development/The World Bank.

more than India's. In spite of the great population differences (Switzerland has a population of seven million versus nearly one billion in India), Switzerland has a larger market for many consumer goods than India; about twice as many passenger cars and many more TVs and telephones. On the other hand, in terms of GDP, India is several times larger than Switzerland and consumes more of the many industrial goods, for example, over three times as many trucks and buses and tons of steel and cement. Obviously, the relevant income figure for evaluating a market will depend on the products involved.

The Nature of the Economy

The economy of a country, like its political, legal, and social systems, is a product of the culture—a part of the distinctive way of life of the people. Though each economy is unique, we can generalize and group them in various ways. The most common way is to group them into developed and developing categories. Other classifications are the *first world*—industrialized West, *second world*—newly industrializing countries, *third world*—developing nations, and *fourth world*—poorest of the developing nations. These designations give some insight, but are only useful in broad terms. We shall not expand on these here because in Chapter 4 we shall see how firms can develop systems for classifying countries in a way most helpful to their own international marketing needs. Here we will identify various features of an economy that constrain a firm's marketing program in a foreign country. The marketer must be alert because many things that are familiar and constant in the domestic market are unfamiliar and variable in foreign markets.

Infrastructure

Infrastructure includes the communications, energy, and transportation facilities in a country. Marketing research and promotion are dependent on the quality of a country's communication facilities. Among the media are the postal service, telephones, print, radio, television, and computer; and as might be expected, their availability varies from country to country. Every nation has a *postal service* but the coverage, frequency, and reliability of mail delivery varies. Much of the world lives in rural areas where mail service is often irregular. In the Democratic Republic of the Congo (formerly Zaire), more or less weekly delivery is the norm. Newspaper circulation varies widely and is especially low in developing countries, in part because of low literacy rates. *Radios* are widespread in all countries and are an ideal medium because they don't depend on literacy. However, not all countries permit commercial messages to be broadcast. *Television* coverage varies greatly between countries and is also limited by restrictions on commercial messages. A notable development has occurred in communist China, however, where western firms are allowed to place commercials on television. The *Internet* is also becoming an important medium, but it relies on access to computers, which sometimes costs more than the average annual income in a given country.

Transportation

The firm's logistics depend upon the country's transportation infrastructure: paved roads, trucks, railroads, and barges. The state of the infrastructure tends to vary according to the nation's level of economic development. Poor countries have relatively weak and inefficient transportation systems, especially outside the cities. The limited nature of these transportation facilities often mean that they are overloaded. A fascinating yet common sight in one of these countries is a train, truck, or bus bursting with humanity, carrying perhaps 50 percent more load than it was designed to accommodate. Contrast that with the United States, where highways are crowded with passenger cars frequently carrying just one person.

The rural population in the majority of developing countries is not served with adequate communications and transportation services. Because of the challenges presented by the lack of a support system, many international marketers confine their efforts to the cities as the only feasible market.

Commercial Infrastructure

Advertising

In addition to communication and transportation facilities, the firm's marketing depends on what we might call the commercial infrastructure: the existence of *advertising agencies,* marketing research firms, and wholesalers and retailers. Not surprisingly, we find great international variation in all these institutions. No country is as supplied with advertising agencies as the United States, though the other industrialized countries are also well served. Advertising's role corresponds roughly to the level of economic development, with some exceptions. Former communist countries are generally in a primitive stage of commercial advertising development. Also, countries at similar income levels may have significantly different levels of advertising expenditure. For example, France spends seven times as much as Belgium. Some poorer countries, on the other hand, spend relatively more than rich countries—Brazil compared to Belgium, for instance. One reassurance for U.S. international marketers is that they are likely to find that the agencies they use at home can be found in many other countries too. Because they follow their larger customers abroad, many advertising agencies have global operations as far-reaching as their clients. McCann-Erickson, for example, does more than half of its business abroad.

Wholesaling

For consumer marketers, wholesalers and retailers are essential ingredients in a marketing program. Their critical role is evident all over the world, but the patterns of wholesale and retail structure are quite diverse.

The role of *wholesalers* in world markets varies between two extremes. In some countries, wholesalers are strong enough to be captain of the channel, having relatively more power than either producer or retailer. They may force private branding on producers and otherwise constrain their marketing efforts. For example, Kraft Foods in Germany designed a program involving efficient direct shipment to retailers. Because of strong wholesaler control over the channel, however, Kraft had to make a payment to wholesalers even though they were not using their services. In countries at the other extreme, wholesalers are small, weak, and dependent. They provide a different constraint by giving limited service and market coverage, and requiring more financing from the producer. Wholesaling tends to vary according to the country's level of development, but some less developed countries have effective wholesaling from the big trading companies. For example, in Africa, many countries enjoy efficient service from United Africa Company, a Unilever subsidiary.

Retailing

Retailing shows diversity similar to that seen in wholesaling. The United States enjoys efficient large-scale retailing with a big volume of sales per outlet and per employee. These figures decline roughly as the per capita income of the country goes down. For example, an African *duka* may have only 200 square feet of floor space, a few shelves and tables for the merchandise, and one employee. Most countries have large numbers of small-scale retailers that limit the product display, product coverage, and other retail services offered. In the United States it is possible for a manufacturer to include a Kroger or Safeway supermarket chain in a special marketing program. The same cannot be done with thousands of small independent retailers. The most extreme fragmentation of retailing is found in those countries where itinerant vendors, on foot or bike, or independent sellers in bazaars constitute major outlets.

Urbanization

International marketers face an easier task in highly urbanized countries than in those where most people live in the countryside. Exhibit 2-6 gives some indication of the international variation. Our word *urbane* comes from *urban* and suggests a noticeable difference between the farmer and the city dweller. In the United States today that difference has been greatly diminished because of modern education, transportation, and communication.

EXHIBIT 2-6   *Variations in Urbanization, 1996*

Highly Urban		Highly Rural	
Country	Percent Urban	Country	Percent Urban
Singapore	100.00	Rwanda	5.80
Kuwait	97.12	Burundi	7.80
Belgium	97.06	Nepal	10.62
Hong Kong, China	95.14	Uganda	12.84
Iceland	91.66	Malawi	13.88
Qatar	91.62	Ethiopia	15.84
Israel	90.80	Papua New Guinea	16.28
Uruguay	90.50	Eritrea	17.42
Germany	86.70	Niger	18.68
Japan	78.26	Vietnam	19.46
United States	76.32	India	27.12
France	74.88	China	31.02

Source: *The World Development Indicators, 1998 CD-ROM,* The International Bank for Reconstruction & Development/The World Bank.

However, in most countries, a different type of consumer as well as a different marketing situation is found in the cities and in the countryside. City dwellers usually have a better education, a higher income, and are dependent upon others for most of their consumption. Country residents on the other hand, supply many of their own needs and wants. Cities are not only concentrated, higher-income markets with people more open to new things, they are also the places with the best infrastructure to facilitate the firm's marketing.

THE PEOPLE ENVIRONMENT

People are obviously the most important part of the environment of marketing. In spite of the common biological characteristics we share as members of the human race, tremendous and fascinating diversity is found among human beings. It makes the world a more interesting place but also complicates efforts such as international marketing. While a travelogue for this topic would be fun, all we can afford is a brief view of the major aspects of our different behaviors, the things a researcher must study to learn about the market. (Buyer behavior is discussed in greater detail in Chapter 3.) People differ in their behavior because most behavior is learned and we have learned it in different environments (cultures) and from different teachers. Culture is the distinctive way of life of a people, it's their distinctive behavior.

CULTURE AS THE SHAPER OF BEHAVIOR

Of the many definitions of culture, we shall discuss only a few to indicate some of the flavor of this complex subject. *Culture* is the distinctive way of life of a people. Culture is the strictly human-constructed aspect of our environment. It is an integrated total pattern of learned behavior shared by members of a society. One could also say that culture is to a society what personality is to an individual.

Marketers are interested in behavior, so international marketers must study culture because culture shapes behavior, including consumer behavior. Culture needs careful study because people are generally unaware of their culture. Normal behavior for a society is not determined by nature but by culture. Culture then is a more or less unconscious part of our life. We behave in ways we consider normal and natural but we are not doing what comes naturally, we are doing what comes culturally. Because we have grown up with it since birth, it is the only behavior we know and we consider it natural and normal. People in other societies consider their "different" behavior also to be normal and natural. In both cases, the behavior is indeed normal, but because of culture, not nature.

The fish is at home in, and comfortably unconscious of, its environment, which is water. The fish only becomes uncomfortable and aware of its environment when it is out of the water. In the same way, we are comfortably unaware of our cultural environment until we leave it and enter another culture. Then we, like the fish, experience what we call *culture shock*. Culture shock is the malaise we feel when we discover that there are different behaviors and values that others accept, practice, and consider normal. We find ourselves unsure of the "right" way to behave.

In international marketing, each foreign market exists within a culture and with behavior different from the firm's home market, and therefore, the marketing situation and task will be different. Not only does each country have a unique culture, most countries also have various subcultures, usually based on ethnicity, religion, or race. Frequently, the various subcultures will indicate differing market segments requiring a separate marketing approach, just as U.S. firms may have a separate director for regional marketing or marketing to minority groups—or in Canada, a separate marketing director for French- and English-speaking Canadians.

Culture is a complex totality of behavior and values and is difficult to examine in its entirety. A convenient way to get a handle on cultural differences is to examine the various dimensions of culture, such as language, religion, values, social organization, and the political and legal systems. We will take that approach here.

Language

A language is not a universal passport but a means of communication *within* a culture. Language differences are important to many communications decisions in marketing, which range from the choice of a brand name or the text for a label or service manual, to promotional messages in advertising or personal selling. Linguists have identified at least 3,000 languages in the world, which means 3,000 different cultures. This multiplicity of language fragments the international marketing effort. Not only does each country usually have its own language, but many countries have several languages. The Democratic Republic of the Congo has more than 100 tribal languages, and the small nation of Singapore has four official languages: English, Malay, Mandarin, and Tamil. One might think the problem is simplified because English or French is an official language in some fifty countries. Unfortunately, most of these nations are former colonies where the majority of the people do not speak the colonial language. For example, in India most of the people do not speak English.

Language not only identifies a cultural group, but also separates it from others. In fact, political scientists use linguistic diversity as a measure of political stability. As an example, French-speaking Quebec talked about seceding from English-speaking Canada. In Belgium, the hostility between French and Flemish speakers is so great that in the Belgian navy, commands are given in English. This complex element of environment does not imply that the international marketer must be a linguist, though language skills are helpful. No individual can master more than a few languages in any case, so the firm must rely on foreign nationals to bridge the language and cultural gaps. Local or expatriate bilingual managers are needed in each foreign subsidiary. Beyond employing multilingual managers, the firm will need to rely on a national agency for its advertising, national distributors to deal with the consumer, and national staff in its salesforce. Of course, language problems are multiplied in multilingual societies, which constitute a majority of the world's nations.

Religion, Values, and Attitudes

Religion is a mainspring of behavior and the basis for most of our values and attitudes. The international marketer needs some knowledge of the religious traditions of a country to understand the behavior of consumers there. The term *Protestant ethic* is used in the West to describe certain people's attitudes toward achievement and work. In a similar fashion, religion is also a factor in attitudes toward acquisition and patterns of consumption. At the most elementary level it can mean periods of abstinence (the month of Ramadan in Islam), avoidance of certain products (pork for Jews and Muslims, beef for Hindus), and high consumption connected with religious holidays (Christmas for Christians). At a broader level it can mean a negative attitude toward acquisition and consumption (in Buddhism, "suffering is caused by desire") or a favoring of traditional patterns of consumption, as in Islam. A dramatic example of the latter is Iran, but the same consumption behavior is seen in Libya and other conservative Muslim nations.

When a country is called Buddhist or Christian or Muslim, it does not mean that everyone in the country is a practitioner of that faith. It means that that religion has left its stamp on their attitudes and behavior. For example, Japan, Hong Kong, Korea, Singapore, and Taiwan are called post-Confucian societies. Although most of the people in these countries are not practicing Confucianists, residual Confucian attitudes toward achievement, work, family, and country explain in significant part these countries' rapid climb toward mass production and mass consumption.

Social Organization

Social organization refers to the *roles* played by individuals and groups in a society and the *relationships* between these individuals and groups. Many of the different kinds of groups in a country are of potential interest to an international marketer: the family, tribe, or other racial or ethnic groups, caste or class. Also, special interest groups, such as unions, consumer groups, Sierra Club, and the National Organization for Women, need consideration. The roles played by male and female, old and young, are part of a social organization, as is the urban-rural division of the country. Each country's unique social organization must be studied to answer marketing questions such as, Who are the relevant reference groups or peer groups? What constitutes a household? What is the buyer decision-making unit?

Family

The family is the basic unit in all societies, but its composition varies. In rich industrial countries the nuclear family, the parents and their children, is the rule. In countries further down on the scale of development, one finds extended family groups, which in a very poor country may number as many as a couple hundred members. The extended family includes three or four generations and cousins, uncles, and aunts. Determining the household or purchasing unit and measuring its buying power or decision influences are quite different in an extended family situation than in the United States. A dramatic example of the relation between the economy and family size is Japan. During the booming decade of the 1960s in Japan, the average family or household size declined from 4.5 members to 3.7 members, down almost 20 percent. Increasing affluence allowed many grandparents to move into separate homes of their own.

Ethnic Groups

Tribal or other ethnic divisions are common to most countries. Every nation has minority groups of some kind. In Africa, tribal divisions frequently have some degree of hostility between them. While this rivalry may not erupt into a conflict like the Biafran war, nonetheless, different tribes may represent different marketing segments. In the United States, Caucasians, African-Americans, and Hispanics often represent distinct target markets that require specialized programs. In Belgium, it is the Flemish versus the Walloons. In most of Latin America, native Indians are a segment separate from the European immigrant population. The reader could cite his or her own examples for other countries. The relevance for the international marketer is that each country has its own combination of groups, each of which require adaptation in marketing programs.

In the '90s, the segmenting or divisive power of ethnicity was obvious around the world. The Soviet Union split into a commonwealth of states, and many of the states are still divided by ethnic rivalries. Yugoslavia fragmented initially into Slovenia and Croatia with continued conflict between Serbs and Croatians and other ethnic groups in the country. Even France and Germany have conflicts with "foreigners" and North African immigrants. In Africa, Somalia, Ethiopia, and Sudan are split along ethnic lines along with much of sub-Saharan Africa. The Kurds are a troubled people, not only in Iraq but also in Iran and Turkey. The Tamils fight the Sinhalese in Sri Lanka, and Malaysia passes a Bumiputra law separating Malay from Chinese Malaysians.

Social Class

Caste and social class usually represent nonethnic divisions in a society. Though the basis for the division is different, the impact on marketing is the same—the creation of market segments. Caste is a rigid social structure based on Hinduism and found in India. Social class is more flexible but is one aspect of social organization in all countries, even in so-called classless societies in communist countries. Varied criteria are used to define social class, but education, income, and occupation are usually included.

Though our overview of social organization must be brief, we can't neglect some of its other dimensions. One is the *role of older people* in the market. What we call *senior citizens* are called *wazee* in Swahili, and other names elsewhere. As their names differ, so does their impact in the market place. Their impact takes one form where older people live in separate households, and another form where they are part of an extended family. Another dimension is the *role of children.* The United States is at one extreme here in this regard; children receive a lot of attention in the marketing activities of many firms. Children are pretty much ignored by marketers in most other countries, even though the 0–14 age group is relatively far larger in many parts of the world. Yet another important dimension is the differential *male-female* role in marketing. Women play somewhat different roles in each culture, and this situation is reflected in the attention marketing gives them, whether they are seen as workers, respondents in a market survey, consumer decision-makers, or shoppers. A final dimension of social organization that is important for marketing is the *urban-rural split,* which has already been discussed.

The many dimensions of social organization add complexity to international marketing. Not only must marketers consider the many foreign markets, but also the several kinds of groupings or market segments within each one. It is a basic challenge of international marketing management. The experienced manager learns to look for international similarities through comparative analysis of markets. Through this process, the fascinating diversity of foreign markets is less likely to become a maze of confusion for the marketer.

THE POLITICAL AND LEGAL ENVIRONMENT

Taking our discussion of the international political environment one step further, we will now consider the *domestic* political influences on the firm in a foreign market. One concern is the political stability of the country. Political unrest and rapid change create a climate of uncertainty typically unfavorable for business. Another cause for concern is the regime that is communist, anticapitalist, or merely xenophobic. For example, few foreign firms operate in Iran or in Castro's Cuba. During the rule of Allende in Chile, Ford, General Motors, and many other U.S. firms left the country. Many returned when a new, more conservative government came to power. A further concern is situations in which a firm is identified by its national origin. This association can be good or bad depending on the relations between the home and host governments. Because of the large and frequently controversial role the United States often plays in the world economy, it has many enemies as well as many friends abroad. Countries that dislike the United States are not particularly appreciative of U.S. goods either. On the other hand, marketers from smaller, less controversial countries such as Sweden or Switzerland are less likely to become political targets.

The political vulnerability of a firm's marketing abroad depends on several things. One is the *political stability* of the host country itself. Another is the *nationality* of the firm. As noted, U.S. firms are particularly vulnerable, and some U.S. firms are symbols of their country abroad. Anger at some U.S. government action or statement might result in the bombing of a local Sears store or Coca-Cola bottling plant. Some *products* are more politically sensitive than others. Pharmaceuticals are particularly vulnerable to attack. Generally, consumer goods are more sensitive than industrial goods, and finished goods more than materials or components, so General Foods and General Motors are more vulnerable than Bendix or TRW. Vulnerability increases with the *size* and *visibility* of the firm in the foreign market. Larger firms are more vulnerable because their size and success may cause resentment of them as foreigners, or "imperialists." Visibility depends partly on size and partly on the advertising and branding policies of the firm. Big advertisers are well known, and international firms usually use advertising more than local firms do. International, rather than local, brand names will often carry more prestige. At the same time, they highlight the foreignness of the product. In Latin America, the name Kodak was successful. However, Eastman Kodak removed Kodak

BOX 2-2 *Just When You Thought It Was Safe, the Rules Change*

It's a market of nearly 200 million people with a GDP growth rate that has been in the 6 to 7 percent range. The country has been under the same leadership for three decades. Labor is cheap; the nation has many natural resources, including rubber, oil, and tin; and it is strategically located between Australia and the Asian mainland. From a business perspective, it is an ideal market. It is Indonesia in the mid-1990s.

For 30 years, if you wanted to do business in Indonesia, you were expected to go through President Suharto, his children, or friends. Privileges included tax-exempt status, bestowed for example on Indonesia's national car company, coincidentally run by Suharto's son. To gain these favors, firms were expected to pay "consulting fees," make "donations," or hire friends and relatives.

Geographically, Indonesia is located in an area that is susceptible to seismic and volcanic activity. But in 1998, it was the people, not the ground that erupted.

An extended drought and uncontrollable forest fires caused prices for food and other basic necessities to rise dramatically. A 70 percent decline in the value of the rupiah (mid-1997 to mid-1993), slower GDP growth rates, bank failures, and an increasing disparity between rich and poor ultimately led to riots, looting, and killing. In the fire that destroyed the Riady mall, at least 79 people died and 20,000 people lost their jobs.

When the smoke from the burning buildings began to clear, thousands of ethnic Chinese and foreigners had abandoned their homes and businesses and fled the country. On May 21, 1998, Suharto stepped down as president.

Formerly invaluable assets—friendships with Suharto kin and cronies—are turning into liabilities. The rules are changing. The political risk is not just a fear of expropriation, but the loss of favorable treatment and the likely enactment of new laws that will affect the profitability of many firms.

Source: "Book of the Year (1998): World Affairs: Indonesia" *Britannica Online* <http:www.eb.com:180/cgi-bin/g?DocF=boy/98/L04140.html> *Washington Post* (May 16, 1998), C1; *Straits Times* (Singapore), (June 1, 1998), 18.

from the corporate name of its subsidiaries after leftist guerrillas kidnapped a director of Kodak Argentina and received $1.5 million in ransom. Kodak wanted a less obviously foreign corporate image.

A negative political environment can have several different results for the firm in a foreign market. It may encounter restrictions on its marketing program or product line. It may have difficulty obtaining permits to operate or to remit profits. It may encounter boycotts or bombings or kid-napping of local managers. The ultimate threat, of course, is expropriation and expulsion. Because all these actions threaten the profitability of the marketing program, the international marketer will find political intelligence an essential ingredient in planning.

The Law

The law represents the written or formal expression of the political will of the nation. In that sense, the political and legal systems of a country are closely related. As a product of its culture, each country's legal system differs somewhat from that of every other country. Legal systems can be classified, however, into four major categories according to their major emphasis: civil or code law systems (about 70 countries), common law systems (about 25 countries), Muslim law systems (about 30 countries), and communist law countries (about 12 countries). Relatively few countries have pure systems; they are usually somewhat of a mixture. The former communist countries in Europe are adopting new legal systems. Their form will become visible as we move into the twenty-first century.

In each foreign country a marketer must consider the legal constraints in designing the marketing program. Few countries will have anything resembling the Robinson-Patman Act or the Clayton Act, but all will have food and drug laws and regulations on the four Ps of marketing: price, product, promotion, and place/distribution. Unfortunately for the marketer, each country has somewhat different laws covering the same marketing activity. Even in the European Union, neighboring member countries are not identical in their marketing regulations. Consider some examples of international differences in marketing regulation:

- Regarding *distribution,* France has a law against door-to-door selling, but in Japan, Avon can operate pretty much as in the United States. In Muslim countries, a traveling vendor would not be allowed to see the woman of the house.
- Most countries have actual or potential government price controls, but they differ in the product coverage. For example, at one time Mexico reduced a list of price controlled products from 274 to 64 (mostly essential consumer goods or industrial materials). At about the same time, the government of France enforced a reduction of five percent in the price of 247 pharmaceuticals.

- *Advertising* is subject to varied regulations around the world. In some countries, radio and TV commercials are not allowed. More than 24 countries have mandatory preclearance of advertisements for pharmaceuticals. A number of developing nations (Egypt, India, Kenya, etc.) have mandatory screening for commercials shown in cinemas.
- As in the United States, most countries are increasing legal specifications on *products*. A prosecutor in Genoa ordered the seizure of all Coca-Cola bottles in Italy because the contents were listed on the cap rather than the bottle. Britain kept French milk off its counters by requiring milk to be sold in pints rather than metric measures. German noise standards kept British lawn mowers off German lawns. As these examples show, national product standards often act to protect national producers as much as national consumers.

SUMMARY

In this chapter, we introduced the environment of international marketing. Many of the topics mentioned are discussed in courses such as anthropology, economics, or political science. We have tried to provide some of the flavor of that environment and to suggest how it differs from the environment facing the domestic marketer. The international marketer would need to study this topic in much greater detail. Building on this background in international and foreign environments, Chapter 3 focuses on the behavior of consumers in foreign markets.

QUESTIONS

1. What is the relationship between international trade and international marketing?
2. Identify the various factors affecting the maintenance and growth of international trade.
3. Describe how the activities of the International Monetary Fund can influence the environment of international marketing.
4. Do the same for the World Trade Organization (WTO).
5. Describe how international politics can affect international marketing.
6. What are the uses and limitations of per capita income figures in evaluating market potential in world markets?

7. Discuss how a country's infrastructure can constrain a firm's marketing there.
8. How does the degree of urbanization in a country affect a firm's marketing?
9. Discuss the impact of language differences on the firm's international marketing.
10. Identify some of the differences in the legal environment in world markets.

FURTHER READING

1. Axtell, Roger E., *Gestures: The Do's and Taboos of Body Language Around the World* (New York: Wiley, 1998).
2. Cateora, Philip R. and John L. Graham, *International Marketing,* 10th ed. (Boston, MA: Irwin/McGraw-Hill, 1999), Chapters 3–7.
3. Ferraro, Gary P., *The Cultural Dimensions of International Business,* 3rd ed. (Upper Saddle River, NJ: Prentice Hall, 1998).
4. Jain, Subhash C., *International Marketing Management,* 5th ed. (Cincinnati, OH: South-Western College Publishing, 1996), Chapter 6–9.
5. Terpstra, Vern, and Kenneth David, *The Cultural Environment of International Business,* 3rd ed. (Cincinnati, OH: South-Western Publishing Company, 1991).
6. Terpstra, Vern, and Ravi Sarathy, *International Marketing,* 7th ed. (Fort Worth, TX: Dryden Press, 1997), Chapters 2–5.

NOTES: Basic marketing texts usually devote several chapters to the environment of marketing. Basic texts in international economics cover extensively the international economic dimensions.

Foreign Consumers and Foreign Markets

All consumers in the world share certain needs and desires. They show however, remarkable diversity in the way they satisfy these needs and desires. No needs are more basic than the needs for food, clothing, and shelter, but the variety in how they are satisfied delights (and occasionally baffles) tourists as they travel the globe. What is fun for the tourist, however, can be a problem for the international marketer. How can one understand buyer behavior when it comes in so many different patterns? Understanding the consumer is difficult enough in the confines of a single country. Can one understand the consumers in 100 or more different world markets?

FOREIGN CONSUMER MARKETS

How Foreign Consumers Differ

Exhibit 3-1 shows a simplified view of the buying decision process. It suggests that the consumer/buyer goes through a complex and only partially understood process called the buying decision. This process is influenced by many different social and personal factors, some of which are indicated

BOX 3-1   *Asia's New Consumers*

Wage earners in Africa, Latin America, and Asia are making more money in real terms. An emerging and growing middle class in many of the world's developing countries is expected to lead to ever-increasing demand for a wide variety of consumer goods. Easier access to telecommunications hardware and software, as well as rising entrepreneurial attitudes in formerly socialist economies, are reasons cited for these changes. Shifting patterns of trade are forecast. Attempts to market to these hungry new consumers require a good deal of care, however.

A recent survey conducted by Grey Advertising highlighted some interesting patterns in Chinese consumer behavior that were contrary to popular conceptions.

- Consumers tend to be brand conscious; they like new products and are willing to try them.
- Most city dwellers already possess large ticket items such as refrigerators, televisions, and washing machines, and are not interested in replacement purchases.
- They are "leap-frogging" products, bypassing VCRs and snapping up DVDs, for example.
- Chinese consumers prefer Chinese products to foreign-made goods.

Ample opportunities await marketers of consumer goods in other Asian nations. Good prospects can also be found in Malaysia, Myanmar (Burma), Cambodia, and Vietnam.

Sources: Trish Saywell, "Curious in China," *Far Eastern Economic Review*, Interactive Edition (July 9, 1998) <http://www.feer.com>; Kathleen Martin, "Worldly Desires," *International Business* (January–February 1998), pp. 10–11.

in the shaded box. The outcome of this process is the purchase, or nonpurchase, of the product being considered. We have reason to believe that this simple model applies to consumers in most countries of the world. Because the influence of family, social class, tastes, and attitudes differ from one country to another, however, the actual buying *behavior* will also differ even though the buying decision *process* is similar.

Foreign consumers differ from domestic consumers in some degree on all aspects of buyer behavior. Foreign consumers differ in *what* they buy, *why* they buy, *who* makes the purchase decision, *how* they buy, *when* they buy, and finally, *where* they buy. What we are saying is not just that U.S.

EXHIBIT 3-1 *A View of the Buying Decision Process*

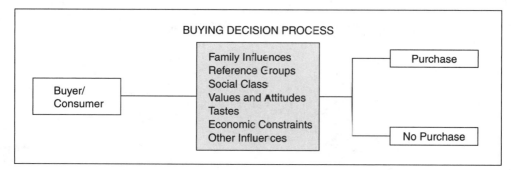

consumers are different from consumers in the rest of the world, but that consumers in each country are different from consumers in every other country. Such a statement does not deny the many similarities in human behavior, and therefore consumer behavior, from country to country. Instead, it recognizes the possibility of international market segments, say, perhaps the jet set whose behavior might be similar from country to country in some aspects.

Two points must be emphasized here. First, consumer behavior is culture bound and thus differs from country to country, and even among subcultures within a single country. The latter idea is well recognized in U.S. marketing, for example, where firms have special programs for ethnic or racial subcultures. The second point is that international *differences* in buyer behavior rather than similarities pose stumbling blocks to successful international marketing. Thus the differences must receive disproportionate attention from the marketer.

What They Buy

People everywhere buy products or services to meet food, shelter, and clothing needs, as well as to satisfy other desires. The things they buy can be classified as durable goods, nondurable goods, and services just as in U.S. marketing. The exact contents of the particular market basket, however, will differ from country to country. Exhibit 3-2 illustrates some differences in selected foreign markets.

The concern of the firm interested in international marketing is whether its products can find a place in the market basket of a particular group of foreign consumers. That concern can be answered by market

EXHIBIT 3-2 *International Variation in Consumption*

Country	Personal Computers (per 1000)	Mobile Phones (per 1000)	Television Sets (per 1000)	Daily Newspapers (per 1000)	Electricity Consumption (kWh/capita)
Argentina	25	9.9	347	138	1,519
Brazil	13	8.3	250	45	1,610
India	1	0.1	61	*	339
Mexico	26	7.6	193	113	1,305
Nigeria	*	0.1	55	18	85
Russian Federation	18	0.6	384	267	4,172
Slovak Republic	41	2.3	380	256	4,075
Turkey	12	7.0	240	44	1,057
United Kingdom	171	98.0	612	351	5,081
United States	328	128.4	806	228	11,570

Source: *World Development Indicators 1998*, CD-ROM, The International Bank for Reconstruction and Development/World Bank.
*Data not available.

research, the topic of Chapter 4. The firm can take initial encouragement, however, from the hundreds of consumer marketers already operating in world markets. Some idea of the wide range of products covered is indicated by the following brief list of international consumer goods marketers: Coca-Cola, Culligan, General Electric, Gillette, General Foods, General Motors, Hamilton Beach, Holiday Inn, Maidenform, and Manhattan Shirt Co. Among non-U.S. firms are Nestle, Philips, Sony, Toyota, and Volkswagen.

Successes and Failures

Not every product introduced abroad by international marketers is a success, of course. A look at a few failures and successes may be insightful.

- General Mills tried to introduce its U.S. cake mixes into England. After a great deal of effort, it was finally forced to take its losses and withdraw.
- Campbell Soup Co. tried to introduce its U.S.-style tomato soup into European markets. After struggling for several years, Campbell decided to introduce European-style tomato soups.
- Coca-Cola has been successful in almost every country of the world by following the same strategy that was unsuccessful for General Mills and Campbell in introducing a U.S. product abroad.
- Kellogg's Corn Flakes has also been successful in many world markets even though it is basically a U.S. product.

Here we have two failures and two successes from firms following the same strategy of carrying their U.S. product into foreign markets. What is the difference? The major problem tripping up both General Mills and Campbell Soup was the fact that cakes and soups were old familiar products with well-established cultural patterns and tastes. The task of changing, or reeducating, the consumer was more difficult and costly than the firms could bear. By contrast, Coca-Cola and Kellogg's Corn Flakes were both new product types to foreign consumers, so the product faced no costly battle of reeducation and no established direct competitors.

Why They Buy

For one person to explain exactly why another person does anything is a problematic task. Nevertheless, anthropologists, psychologists, sociologists, novelists, and marketers all work at explaining other people's behavior with varying degrees of success. Part of their success comes from their scientific methods, and part of it derives from the common human nature the researcher shares with all humankind. These researchers have designed various models to explain buyer behavior. Although many of these models were designed in the United States, some would have value in foreign countries because the researchers have learned to ask the right questions. It should be noted, however, that most of these models have not been tested empirically in foreign countries or even in the United States. One of the examples we can cite here is Maslow's hierarchy of needs model, shown in Exhibit 3-3. Maslow suggested that primary needs (hunger, thirst, sex, and survival) must be met first, but once they are satisfied, higher level needs (self-esteem, self-actualization) play a major role in behavior. Maslow's model presumably applies to consumer buying behavior in many different countries, but its relevance has yet to be proven.

We have mentioned that we share certain characteristics with people in all other countries because of our common membership in the human race. This fact does not mean that buyer behavior and motivation are the same in different countries. Buyer behavior is not instinctive but learned, and therefore culturally determined. Culture is the distinctive way of life of a people; thus, buyer behavior also varies from country to country or, more accurately, from culture to culture, because many countries have more than one culture.

A certain model may tell us how values and attitudes act as determinants of buyer behavior. In all countries values are mainsprings of behavior. The actual values affecting consumer behavior, however, will be unique to the culture, typically influenced by the religion of the culture. As one extreme example, the devout Buddhist is a resistant target of marketing activity. The Noble Truths of Buddhism state that human suffering is caused by desire and that Nirvana is achieved in part by the absence of desire. As another example, the traditional devout Muslim does not share

EXHIBIT 3-3   *Hierarchy of Needs Model*

1. Physiological needs such as hunger, thirst, and sex
2. Safety or survival needs
3. Needs for love and affection
4. Needs for self-esteem and respect from others
5. Self-actualization needs

Source: A. H. Maslow, *Motivation and Personality* (New York: Harper & Row, Publishers, 1954).

the American enthusiasm for new or foreign goods and services. Mohammed said, "All innovation is of the Devil." The Taliban religious army in Kabul reiterated that idea, rejecting many western innovations in Afghanistan. More dramatically, the youth in many Muslim countries have joined in the resurgence of conservatism, throwing out their television sets, VCRs, and satellite dishes, and the women dropping out of the universities to resume their traditional role and garb.

Another model may explain how social class and reference groups determine U.S. consumer behavior. This situation will also be true in other countries, but the social class or caste or tribe that is important will vary by country. Social classes and pecking orders are culture created. Reference groups are also culturally distinctive. For example, in many former colonies the Europeans were an important reference group for consumer behavior. After independence some of the countries were resentful of the former colonizers, who came to be seen in a negative light. This changing role of a reference group was observed during eight years in the Democratic Republic of the Congo.

> A changing reference group situation is occurring in Korea. The resentment toward the Japanese resulted from their brutal occupation of Korea during the first half of the twentieth century. Japanese movies, music, and magazines were all banned in Korea. Now, however, Japanese culture is increasingly appealing to certain groups in Korea. Korean students are flocking to Japanese language lessons, while Japanese music and magazines are smuggled into Korea and sold openly.
>
> The debate over lifting the ban on Japanese goods that are cultural in nature continued into mid-1998. Other positive signs are emerging. President Kim Dae-jung stated he would consider removing the ban on Japanese karaoke videos and the South Korean cultural authorities granted permission to perform a Japanese-language play in Seoul, although they did ban the playing of Japanese music during the performance.[1]

Who Makes the Purchase Decision

In U.S. marketing the person who influences or decides upon a consumer purchase generally depends on the product being bought and the family situation. Differing roles will be identified for parents, children,

---

[1]"Perfect Harmony," *The Financial Times* (April 6, 1998), p. 5; "Theater Group to Tour South Korea," *Mainichi Daily News* (May 27, 1998), 12.

husbands, and wives. Because a similar diversity will be found in foreign countries, it is difficult to generalize about consumer decision making abroad. We can make a couple of observations, however. One pertains to the *role of children,* who generally play a lesser role in consumer decision making than they do in the United States. In most countries children are minors not only in a legal sense, but are also considered minors in terms of family decision making. The values in these societies place greater weight on the worth of age and experience than they do on the rights and wisdom of children.

The second observation pertains to the *role and structure of the family.* As mentioned earlier, in the United States family includes the parent(s), and their children who live at home. The average family size is about three or four members. In developing countries, one typically finds the extended family, which will have many more members. The extended family is a social, political, and economic unit. Part of the rationale is to provide various kinds of security to its members, things provided by the government in the United States, for example. Many societies are patriarchal, and some revere their elders and the wisdom that comes with age. In these cultures, older males typically have an important voice in consumption decisions, which means a lesser voice for others.

How They Buy

All around the world consumer buying can be considered a problem-solving activity. In all countries, purchasing situations can be classified into three categories: (1) routine buying, requiring little thought or effort, (2) limited problem solving, requiring more information search and more time, and (3) extensive problem solving, a more complex situation for the buyer involving still more information, time, and effort. Because the products facing each of these buying situations will vary somewhat from country to country, the firm may need market research to determine the marketing task it will face.

Another way of looking at how consumers buy is to consider the steps in the buying process. First is need arousal. The consumer becomes aware of *something* of potential interest. Second is the information search. The consumer finds out more about that *something.* Third is evaluation behavior. Using personal criteria, the consumer weighs the feasibility and desirability of having *something.* Fourth is the decision to buy. Based on the evaluation in step three, the consumer buys (or does not buy) *some-*

thing. Fortunately, these steps are suitable for studying buyer behavior in all countries. As one might expect, however, the cues that trigger need arousal, the nature of and the sources in the information search, and the evaluation process will all be variable internationally, and therefore, the purchase decision will also differ.

When They Buy

The *when* of international consumer buying varies in several dimensions. Frequency of purchase is one. In some countries grocery shopping may be done daily versus once or twice a week in the United States. Car buying may be done every few years in some countries, but once in ten years or a lifetime or even never in others. Another variable is the time of day. Consumer preferences and availability are factors as to when shopping is done. Another factor is vendor availability. In the United States, it is possible to shop for many items 24 hours a day, seven days a week. In some countries, markets may be open only one or two hours a day or only one or two days a week.

The time of the month or the time of the year is another variable affecting the marketing of certain products. Climate is one obvious influence; consider temperate versus tropical zones and Northern versus Southern hemispheres. Religious holidays are equally important, Christmas, Ramadan, the Chinese New Year. for example. A final aspect as to when consumers buy is the fact that some products may be purchased at a different part of the individual or family life cycle in different countries.

The following example is not typical in that it represents expatriate, rather than national buyer behavior. It is useful, however, in identifying certain aspects of the timing and other dimensions of consumer behavior in a developing country, the Democratic Republic of the Congo.

> During their years spent in the Congo, one U.S. family's consumer buying—the timing and pattern of it—was quite different from what it had been in the United States. Certain fresh fruits and vegetables were home grown and did not enter the market. Fresh meat was bought when a hunter had some game he was willing to sell. Water was obtained on a daily basis by hiring someone to go to the spring and fill the water drums. Wood for fuel was purchased weekly by hiring someone to go to the forest and cut a week's supply. Several years' supply of standard clothing items was brought from the United States, but it was supplemented on a regular basis as needed by buying cloth and hiring a local tailor to make suits, shirts, dresses, and so forth.

Several items of consumption were not available in the surrounding economy. For these items, a two-day shopping trip four times a year to a city about six hours away was necessary. Items included canned foods, powdered milk, rice, flour, sugar, and medicines as well as a supply of gasoline. These items are bought on a weekly basis in the States (except for medicines).

The consumer behavior of the Congolese had several similarities. First, most items of food and shelter were self-supplied and didn't enter the market economy. Things bought on a regular basis in the market place included soap, salt, sugar, kerosene, and flashlight batteries. Because most did not have a regular weekly income, they had to wait for the annual cash crop for the bulk of their purchasing power. Thus, their major purchases were made around the time of the year when the cash crop was sold. These purchases included clothing, furniture, bikes, watches, sewing machines, and radios. This constraint on the timing of these major purchases was occasionally modified by credit extension by local merchants.

Where They Buy

Where consumers buy depends on the marketing outlets available to them. In some countries, a consumer can buy a given item in a drug store, supermarket, gas station, discount store, department store, by mail order, or over the Internet. Consumers generally exhibit distinct national preferences as to the favored store for different kinds of products. For example, the British buy more than half of their clothing in multiple chain stores such as Marks and Spencer, whereas the French buy only four percent of their clothing in such stores. The Germans buy one-fourth of their domestic appliances via mail order versus just over one percent for the Dutch.

The variety of retail outlets in world markets is fascinating. In some countries, itinerant vendors on foot or bike and colorful public markets and bazaars are major retailers. In other countries, retail patterns would be somewhat more like those in the United States, including the vending machine. Regardless of surface similarities, the international marketer will find that retailing is culturally distinctive, varying from country to country. We shall discuss this topic more in Chapter 6, International Distribution Decisions.

FOREIGN INDUSTRIAL MARKETS

A significant part of international trade concerns the various nonconsumer markets abroad: industrial, governmental, and special market situations. Foreign industrial markets reflect the economy and culture that gave them birth. Thus, they exhibit the same diversity we saw in consumer markets. The differences are probably somewhat less pronounced because of the greater international similarity in buying motives in the industrial market. Industrial markets abroad differ on two dimensions, *size* and *nature* of the national industrial structure. Size differences do not mean merely that some countries are bigger than others are, but rather those countries with similar population size will have vastly different amounts of industry.

The countries of the European Union (EU) average about 20 percent of their domestic product in manufacturing, 70 percent in services, and less than 5 percent in agriculture. India and the countries of Africa average 13 percent in manufacturing, and 45 percent in agriculture. It can be seen why the developing nations are also called nonindustrial or agrarian countries.[2]

Each country will also differ in the nature of its industrial structure. Countries that do have manufacturing sectors will have different industry profiles. Probably no other economy has as complete and complex an industrial structure as the United States, producing everything from automobiles to aircraft, chemicals to computers, earthmovers to electric furnaces, shoes to steel, and textiles to television equipment. Other countries do not have all these industries, and some have few at all. A second level of difference in industrial markets is the degree of sophistication in industrial equipment and processes. Producers in various countries often use different methods or production functions to produce the same goods. The general rule is that production becomes more labor intensive as one moves down the scale of economic development.

The agricultural or farm market is one kind of industrial market. It illustrates to an extreme degree the range of variation in production functions, equipment used, and labor intensity. The average American farmer has over $250,000 in capital equipment. This does not include the land or house. In developing countries, a rich farmer might have a pair of oxen and a steel pointed plow, but most subsistence-level farmers won't have anything more than wooden tools, plus perhaps a hoe or machete. They make do with lots of human effort and none of the complex machinery, electric and gas power that the American farmer enjoys.

---

[2]*World Development Indicators 1998, CD-ROM,* The International Bank for Reconstruction and Development/World Bank.

Each country has a unique industrial profile, but recognizable similarities that are evident between countries permit some comparison and classification. The simplest distinction and grouping would be that of industrialized and nonindustrialized countries. More usefully, Rostow has identified five stages of economic development. His categories are based on the nature of the economy and industrial structure and are described in Exhibit 3-4. The countries of the world are found at different levels or stages. A classification system of this type can be helpful for international marketers of industrial goods. Another way to gain insight into the differences in foreign industrial markets is to repeat some of the questions we asked about foreign consumer markets. Here we shall review the what, why, and who of foreign industrial buying behavior.

EXHIBIT 3-4   *Rostow's Stages of Economic Growth*

Stage 1. The Traditional Society
    One with limited production functions, primarily agriculture. The level of productivity in manufacture as in agriculture is limited by the inaccessibility of modern science, its applications, and its frame of mind.

Stage 2. The Preconditions for Take-Off
    Societies in transition toward modernization. Some investment in infrastructure occurs, and there is a widening scope of internal and external commerce. Some modern manufacturing appears, but the society is still mainly characterized by the old social structure and values.

Stage 3. The Take-Off
    Resistance to change lessens, and the forces for economic growth come to dominate the society. Industries expand rapidly, requiring new investment. New techniques spread in agriculture as well as industry.

Stage 4. The Drive to Maturity
    Continuing growth extends modern technology over the whole range of economic activity. The make-up of the economy changes unceasingly as technique improves, new industries grow, and older ones level off. The economy extends its range into more complex technologies.

Stage 5. The Age of High Mass Consumption
    The leading sectors shift toward durable consumers' goods and services. The structure of the working force changes with more employed in offices or in skilled factory jobs. The extension of modern technology as an objective is joined with a desire to improve social welfare and security.

Source: W. W. Rostow, *The Stages of Economic Growth*, 2d ed. (Cambridge: The University Press, 1971).

What They Buy

Industrial goods, that is, goods that will be used in production processes rather than for personal consumption, are purchased everywhere. These goods may be raw materials or components, plant and production equipment, and supplies and services. These categories apply to industrial goods in all countries, but within each category the specific goods and services demanded vary somewhat from country to country. This variety can be seen easily by looking at such a traditional industry as steel. Many countries of the world have a steel industry, but a surprising diversity in all categories characterizes the industrial goods going into it. Even the iron ore and coking fuel will differ, not to mention the physical plant, the furnaces, and the control equipment.

An industrial marketer such as IBM can tell many stories about the international variations in the demand for industrial goods. IBM supplies the same industries—banking, commerce, manufacturing, and transportation—all around the world, but finds adaptation necessary in the products and services it supplies to a given industry in a particular country.

The products that industrial consumers buy vary from country to country for numerous reasons. Economists have written volumes about economic development and international production functions in which they indirectly address this issue. Risking oversimplification, we shall give some summary explanations. The first reason that purchasing behavior varies is that *industrial consumer needs vary.* One factor is *scale of operation.* A firm that produces 500 tires or ten cars each day will need different plant and equipment from one that makes 5,000 tires or 1,000 cars every day. A second factor is *labor costs.* A firm in a country where wages are the equivalent of $25 per week will not need the robots, numerical controls, and other labor-saving devices of a country where wages are the equivalent of $25 per hour.

A second reason for international variations in industrial buying is the *difference in the economic and technical capability of the buyers.* A piece of production equipment or a computer does not function in a vacuum. It is part of a system and is dependent upon other human and material inputs in order to function properly. Precision machinery will not work well with dissimilar inputs or an uneven power supply. Furthermore, if the managers, supervisors, and/or workers do not have the training and skills to work with such machinery, a firm is wasteful in buying it.

Why They Buy

Industrial demand is derived demand; goods are purchased to meet the needs of the production process, the output of which ultimately goes to others. In all countries, the objectives of production lead to a greater similarity in buying motives among industrial buyers than the motives found among individual end-users. In no country is the industrial purchaser completely rational and objective in his or her buying habits. For example, one can find firms everywhere buying, for reasons of status, equipment that is more expensive and sophisticated than they can economically justify. The mix of rationality and subjectivity, however, varies among countries. In some nations, relatively more attention will be paid to the family ties, religion, tribe, or race of the seller. The divisions in the society may be reflected in industrial buying behavior at the expense of economic efficiency. Another international difference is the degree to which bribery and influence peddling play a role in industrial buying.

Who Makes the Purchase Decision

Around the world, industrial buying is generally considered a specialized function or department in the firm. International differences can arise in two areas. One is that in countries with more authoritarian management styles, the chief executive will tend to play a greater role in purchasing decisions. The bigger difference comes from the fact that, compared to the United States, most countries have more small and medium-sized firms with a greater family ownership and influence. In family firms, family members usually control the major purchase decisions, and subjective factors frequently come into play in their decisions. Having the right contacts can be as important as having the right products.

FOREIGN GOVERNMENT MARKETS

Government is the largest buyer of goods and services in every country of the world. The size of the government's role as customer, however, varies from country to country as seen in Exhibit 3-5. It should be noted that those figures only account for *central* government expenditure and therefore understate the total role of governments as customers. A government's role follows no predictable pattern, and one can find wide variation in government consumption at every level of development. The government's role is perhaps easiest to understand in the developing world.

EXHIBIT 3-5   *Governments as Customers (Percent of GDP), 1995*

Country	Central Government Expenditure/GDP
Low Income Countries	Average 20.0%
Sierra Leone	14.8
India	16.4
Nepal	20.1
Zambia	20.8
Burundi	21.9
Sri Lanka	27.4
Lower Middle Income Economies	Average 26.7%
Indonesia	14.7
Thailand	16.1
Peru	16.5
Philippines	18.3
Turkey	26.8
Bulgaria	49.8
Upper Middle Income Countries	Average 31.9%
Chile	19.5
Malaysia	22.0
Mauritius	22.3
Uruguay	33.1
Czech Republic	37.5
Poland	42.1
High Income Countries	Average 36.3%
Korea, Rep. (South)	18.6
United States	22.4
Germany	33.7
France	46.7
Netherlands	48.5
Italy	50.5

Source: The *World Development Indicators 1998 CD-ROM*, The International Bank
for Reconstruction & Development/The World Bank.
Note: Averages are of entire group, not just the countries shown.

Many of the poorer developing countries do not have much of a private sector because much of the population is engaged in subsistence-level agriculture, and therefore, most economic activity falls to the government by default. For example, until recently the Indian government owned the postal, telecommunications, electric, gas, oil, coal, railway, airline, and shipbuilding industries. The central government still owns or has strict controls over many of these industries, but privatization efforts during the mid- and late-1990s have opened the market to local and foreign investors in sectors such as telecommunications and banking. Many countries, not just those that are experimenting with market-driven economics, are actively promoting privatization as an alternative to government monopolies. Argentina, Australia, Brazil, Canada, Chile, Estonia, India, Mexico, Sweden, and Switzerland are a few of the countries seeking ways to privatize intercity rail travel and related industries.

Another variable in the economic role of governments is the *kind of economic activity* undertaken. In Cuba, every factory, hospital, school, and railroad is owned by the people, that is, the government. Other governments are more selective about the activities they control. Even though the military and the postal system are government monopolies everywhere, a mixture of private-government ownership across countries is the case in almost every other activity. Transportation and communications media fall largely within the private sector in the United States, but largely within the governmental sector in many other countries. Education and medical care have varied degrees of private sector participation. Even in these basic services government plays no uniform role. The scenario within other industries is even more varied. In some countries the automobile and steel industries are government owned, while in others they are in the private sector. In France the government is in the tobacco business.

In many countries, governments are beginning to realize that government ownership is not the most efficient way to operate. In many former communist countries the trend has been toward *privatization*—spinning off government-owned businesses to the private sector.

The role of government in an economy is a product of its culture, politics, and history, so each country has a unique pattern of government participation. We have seen some indication of the international variation in this participation. What are the marketing implications?

Government markets differ from consumer and industrial markets in what they buy, how they buy, and why they buy; and governments in different countries also vary among themselves on these dimensions. *What governments buy in all countries are those products and services neces-*

sary to run the government bureaucracy. However, when governments also run a variety of economic enterprises, such as transportation, communications, steel mills, or automobile plants, the range of goods and services purchased will be even greater, covering not only every kind of industrial good but many consumer goods as well.

When it comes to *how* governments buy, they resemble industrial buyers in having some kind of specialized purchasing department and buying according to formal or objective specifications. For example, a pharmaceutical firm faces a different marketing task when the British National Health Service is its only customer rather than in a country where it must promote to thousands of independent doctors. Unfortunately for the international marketer, government purchasing organizations show about as much behavior variation as do consumer and industrial markets abroad. Selling to the French government with its well-developed and highly structured civil service is quite different from selling to Saudi Arabia where the government (a monarchy) is an extended family.

Finally, governments differ in their buying *motivations*. They have specifications about the product or service, but their objective function is unlike the profit maximization of the firm. Therefore, government buyers may show more variation in their behavior than industrial buyers. Some government objectives that may affect its buying behavior are the desires to lessen unemployment, eliminate a balance of payments deficit, or develop national industry. Where the nation is fighting unemployment or a payments deficit, it prefers to buy goods made within the country rather than purchasing imports. This strategy employs nationals and does not require foreign exchange for the purchase. In this case, having the best product is not sufficient. The firm must further arrange for local production in its own facilities or via licensing or joint venture. For example, General Dynamics won a large NATO contract for the F-16 fighter plane only by agreeing to subcontract a share of the production to each of the countries buying the plane roughly proportional to its share of the purchase.

The Los Angeles County Transportation Commission chose Sumitomo to build the railcars for the county's new transit system, even though the American firm Morrison Knudsen had a lower bid. There arose a great public outcry to "Buy American" and save American jobs. After extensive media coverage, the Commission withdrew the contract from Sumitomo and promised that the winner would be required to keep 70 percent of the labor inside the United States and 60 percent within Los Angeles County.

The European Union is implementing new, more liberal national government procurement policies. A firm from one member country could tender for a government contract in another member country. Generally, these new policies do not apply to firms from outside the EU. A substantial local presence may be necessary for marketing to governments.

The Former Communist Countries of Europe

Communist countries were a special subset of government markets abroad because those governments controlled all economic activity and any international marketing required negotiation with the government. With the collapse of communism in eastern Europe and former Soviet states, the countries are in transition to some kind of market-oriented economy. It will take years before the transition is complete. Some western ventures that had dealt with previous government administrations are continuing, such as McDonalds, Pizza Hut, Pepsi-Cola and Levi Strauss. Pizza Hut in Moscow gained tremendous publicity by supplying free pizzas and beverages to Yeltsin and his supporters when they were defying the coup forces trying to depose Gorbachev.

Western firms look hopefully at the potentially large markets of the former communist nations. Many have already taken steps to establish themselves in the market, in spite of the uncertainty. Some examples in place or in process as of 1998 illustrate the breadth and variety of western business interest.

- Gillette is building a US $40 million plant in St. Petersburg to boost production of shaving products.
- American and Russian entrepreneurs have started a bungee-jumping business in Vladivostok called Tarzan Limited.
- Goodyear and Sava (Slovenia rubber group) have agreed to produce tires, transmission belts, air springs, and hoses.
- Ispat International of the United Kingdom has signed on to run the privatized Karmet steel mill in Kazakhstan.
- Ford Motor Company supplies buses for the Moscow transit system from its new Belarus plant.
- Telecommunications privatization in Croatia drew bids from German (Deutsche Telekom), American (MediaOne International), French (France Telecom), and Hungarian (Matav) firms.
- Rio de la Plata (Argentina) is considering a US $40 million cooking oil processing plant near Moscow.
- A joint venture between ITI (Poland) and USI (Paramount and Universal Studios) to open a multiplex theater in Poland.

- A joint venture between Sea-Land Service, Inc. and the Russian Railways Ministry is expected to generate US $90 million.
- A proposal for a French and Russian space program joint venture is in the works.

Because the former communist countries are invariably short of foreign exchange, they often require western sellers to take all or part of their payment in goods instead of money. This practice is called countertrade or barter and effectively makes the western firm the international marketing arm of the eastern supplier. These selling conditions are not preferred by western firms, but many are engaged in this trade because the markets are too large to ignore. The examples of Pepsi-Cola and Levi Strauss illustrate some of the diverse arrangements firms make to get into these markets.

- Pepsi-Cola has been sold in the Soviet Union since 1974. The political aspects are emphasized by the fact that the deal was negotiated by Pepsi president Donald Kendall after he became acquainted with the Soviet leaders during a visit to the Soviet Union with then-president, Richard Nixon—scarcely a typical marketing negotiation. As a result, several Pepsi bottling plants operate in the country, mostly in Russia. The arrangement operates in this way: Pepsi supplies cola syrup to the government, which operates the bottling plants and markets the product with little control from Pepsi. In return, rather than receiving royalties, Pepsi is granted the exclusive U.S. distributorship of Russian-made vodka, Stolichnaya. Thus, as Pepsi sells more Stolichnaya it creates more trade volume for Pepsi that is sold locally, generating more income Pepsi is able to earn from this arrangement.
- Levi Strauss & Co. concluded a five-year agreement with Hungarotex, a Hungarian FTO, providing for the production of Levi's jeans and other apparel in the Majus 1 Ruhagyar clothing factory. Levi Strauss supplies the technology and materials. It also sets up a training program, maintains quality control, and provides design services. The U.S. company takes back 10 percent of the production. The remainder is sold locally (40 percent) and marketed in other countries (50 percent).

Less-Developed Countries

Less-developed countries are another subset of government markets. Because of their poverty and lack of development, they may want special products. They may ask a food processor to develop a low-cost, high-protein food product instead of selling Wheaties or Quaker Oats, or ask an automobile firm to make a sturdy, simple, and inexpensive car instead of a standard Chevrolet. General Motors' in-house name for the vehicle they developed was BTV (basic transportation vehicle). Another reason these governments are different is that they are less experienced and organized for purchasing decisions. Bribery and influence peddling are also likely to be more important in such countries. All these factors combine to create a different challenge in marketing to these governments.

Another reason these governments are a different kind of customer is that precisely because of their poverty, they often provide special marketing opportunities through the financial assistance given to them by the World Bank or the aid programs of other countries. This aid (often in the form of grants or loans) is given to spur the country's development and is often used for major construction projects such as roads, harbors, or dams. However, much of it also goes into other areas of the economy such as agriculture, education, medical care, and tourism, providing marketing opportunities for many different kinds of firms, especially when several billion dollars are spent on such programs each year. The marketing task changes because the suppliers of the grant or loan will also have a voice in the what and where of the purchase decision. A two-sided transaction becomes a three-sided transaction: the firm, the government, and the supplier of funds. Most foreign aid, for example, is tied to purchases in the donor country. In transactions arranged with World Bank financing, the World Bank becomes a major purchase influence and source of product specifications. To take advantage of these opportunities, the marketer may have to deal with two parties, both in terms of market intelligence and in terms of the selling job.

SUMMARY

In spite of the common humanity we all share as members of the human race, great diversity of behavior is found in different parts of the world. This situation exists because culture, rather than physiology, largely determines our behavior. This diversity is fascinating to the observer, but it can also be a problem for the international marketer who must learn how to satisfy customers with widely different buying behaviors. We have given some indication of the differences in the buying behavior of individual consumers, industrial buyers, and government buyers in world markets. We now turn to the question of how the international marketer can learn more about world markets and consumers. We will discuss International Marketing Research in Chapter 4.

QUESTIONS

1. Discuss some of the ways the behavior of consumers abroad may differ from the behavior of consumers in the United States.
2. Why are some U.S. products that have not been adapted still successful abroad, whereas others fail?
3. How can different methods of family organization in world markets cause purchasing behavior to differ from that in the United States?
4. Why do industrial customers in international markets differ in what they buy?
5. Identify some of the variations in government markets around the world.
6. Discuss some of the special aspects of marketing to governments in developing countries.

FURTHER READING

1. Cateora, Philip R. and John L. Graham, *International Marketing,* 10th ed. (Boston, MA: Irwin/McGraw-Hill, 1999), Chapter 9.
2. Craig, Samuel C. and Susan P. Douglas, "Responding to the Challenges of Global Markets: Change, Complexity, Completion, and Conscience," *Columbia Journal of World Business* (Winter 1996), pp. 6–18.
3. Hawkins, Del I., Roger J. Best, and Kenneth A. Coney, *Consumer Behavior: Building Marketing Strategy,* 7th ed. (Boston: McGraw-Hill, 1998), Chapter 2.
4. Mitchell, Vincent W. and Michael Grentorex, "Consumer Purchasing in Foreign Countries." *International Journal of Advertising,* vol. 9, no. 4 (1990), pp. 295–307.
5. Rostow, W. W., *The Stages of Economic Growth,* 2d ed. (Cambridge: The University Press, 1971).
6. Terpstra, Vern, and Kenneth David, *The Cultural Environment of International Business,* 3rd ed. (Cincinnati: South-Western, 1991).

NOTE: Basic marketing texts discuss the nature of consumer behavior and industrial markets in one or more chapters.

CHAPTER 4

International Marketing Research

WHAT IS INTERNATIONAL MARKETING RESEARCH?

Marketing research is the systematic gathering, recording, and analyzing of data to provide information to guide marketing decision making. *International* marketing research has the same function but in a much broader context. The difference lies in the *scope* of the research and the *way it is conducted,* rather than in the role it plays in the firm's marketing.

The *scope* of international marketing research is broader than domestic marketing research in two ways. First, international marketing research may need to be conducted in as many as 150 countries, each of which is unique in varying degrees. This task may sound overwhelming in the amount of diversity it must cover except when one realizes that each of the 50 states in the United States is also unique in certain ways. This comparison is not meant to minimize the difficulty of international marketing research but to suggest that firms are accustomed to dealing with some diversity in their home market, and international marketers can learn to deal with diversity in world markets as well.

A second aspect of the broader scope of international marketing research is the greater range of variables on which data must be gathered.

BOX 4-1   *Primary Data Collection in the Southern Hemisphere*

The financial crisis in Asia in 1997 and 1998 sent shock waves through the rest of the world. In one day of particularly heavy trading, the U.S. stock market recorded more than one billion stock exchanges, and over a 10-day period in August 1998, the market lost 20 percent of its value. In response to shrinking markets in Asia and to meet sales goals, firms turned to Latin American markets, with its half-billion potential customers.

Marketing Development Inc., headquartered in San Diego, and Strategy Resource, located in Miami, are market research companies that specialize in Hispanic consumer research. These and other research firms are following their U.S. customers into Latin America. In 1997, market research spending increased 10 percent in Latin markets, to approximately $465 million. Unlike Asia with its many cultures, researchers can often use the same, or at least similar questionnaires when collecting data in Latin countries.

Research in Latin America is still evolving, however, and researchers face a number of problems. For example, while the population is relatively more receptive to participating in surveys than U.S. citizens, the novelty of participating in research is likely to wear off quickly. Also, many homes do not have telephones, mail service is poor in many areas, and addresses may be nonexistent or hard to obtain, making phone and mail sampling difficult at best.

Despite some commonalities across nations, Portuguese, rather than Spanish is spoken in Brazil, other countries have many local dialects, and companies often use different names for the same product. These distractions mean it is still necessary to carefully translate questionnaires and scrupulously train the surveyors and focus group moderators.

Source: Fellman, Michelle Wirth, "U.S. Market Researchers Follow Their Clients South," *Marketing News*, American Marketing Association (August 17, 1998), p. 15.

Aspects of the home market that are familiar and constant, or changing very slowly—for example, the legal system or distribution channels—become variable in each foreign market. Furthermore, the researcher must study not only the variables within each relevant foreign market but also the international variables that can affect the marketing program, for example, international politics, exchange rates, and so forth. In other words, all the factors we discussed in Chapters 2 and 3 are subjects of international marketing research. Most international marketers have checklists of items on which information is necessary. Many of these lists have six or more headings with 50 or more subheadings. One such list, taken from a text on international marketing, can be found in Exhibit 4-1.

EXHIBIT 4-1   *International Marketing Research Checklist*

---

1. Competition
2. Transportation
3. Other infrastructure
4. Trade barriers
5. The economy
6. Business philosophies
7. Legal system
8. Social customs
9. Languages
10. Political climate
11. Consumption patterns
12. Relevant cultural patterns
13. Religious and moral background
14. Philosophies of major political groups

Source: Cateora, Philip, *International Marketing* (Homewood, Ill.: Richard D. Irwin, 1987), p. 254.

The list in Exhibit 4-1 provides an indication of the kinds of elements to be considered many of which are discussed later in this chapter. Obviously, each firm must specify its own international marketing information needs. These specific needs will vary by firm according to its industry and the size and nature of its international business.

Another way of noting the great coverage of international marketing research is to consider the *kinds of decisions* that will depend on it. Domestic marketing research is aimed at getting information to guide the firm in its marketing program: How should we price our product? What products should we introduce? What is the most effective promotional program? International marketing research tries to obtain information to assist in these same decisions, but for *each* foreign market. In addition to foreign market decisions, and even before they become relevant, three other strategic decisions require international marketing intelligence: (1) Should our firm go international? (2) If the answer is yes, then which foreign markets should we enter? (3) For the chosen target markets, how should we enter those markets, by exporting, licensing, or using our own local subsidiary? The kind of intelligence needed for these decisions is different from that needed to guide the formulation of local marketing programs once the firm has entered the foreign market. Exhibit 4-2 shows the nature of the task.

EXHIBIT 4-2   *The Task of International Marketing Research*

Marketing Decision	Intelligence Needed
1. Go international or remain a domestic marketer?	Assessment of global market demand and firm's potential share in it, in view of local and international competition and compared to domestic opportunities
2. Which markets to enter?	A ranking of world markets according to market potential, local competition, and the political situation
3. How to enter target markets?	Size of market, international trade barriers, transportation and production costs, local competition, government requirements, and political stability
4. How to market in target markets?	For each market: buyer behavior, competitive practice, distribution channels, promotional medic and practice, company experience in local market and in other markets

Exhibit 4-2 describes the general nature of the job facing the international marketing researcher. The exact task varies according to the company and its needs. Along that line, it is useful to consider the following placement notice from Upjohn as an illustration of a specific position in international marketing research.

Position: Marketing Research Analyst—International
Description: Provide assistance in solving marketing problems and supporting marketing activities by gathering, analyzing, and interpreting data. Assist in sales forecasting, budgeting, and long-range planning. Responsible for assisting marketing planning for specific product groups and for analyses of foreign markets. Some international travel.

Conducting International Marketing Research

We have seen some of the information requirements for making international marketing decisions. How do firms go about getting this information? The first three decisions (go international, which markets to enter, and how to enter) have no direct counterpart in domestic marketing research. What is needed for these decisions is more related to international economic and political intelligence than traditional market research. By contrast, the fourth decision, choosing marketing programs for foreign markets, involves much the same research procedures the firm uses at home, although these procedures encounter certain difficulties abroad. Our approach here will be to take each of the international marketing decision areas and to suggest information sources and research approaches. Our discussion will be only indicative. A primer on international marketing research would be a book unto itself. In fact, John Kracmar who worked for Singer wrote a whole book on the subject regarding developing countries alone. Douglas and Craig also authored a textbook on this subject. (These references and others are included in the readings list at the end of the chapter.)

The Decision to Go International

Because international business entails difficulties and risks not found domestically, the firm should carefully consider its prospects before venturing abroad. It should be mentioned here that only a small percentage of U.S. firms have gone international, either because they are being cautious or, more likely, they are ignorant of foreign market opportunities. The primary information source for the decision to go international is the assessment of global *demand* and *competition*. The ease of this assessment varies by industry.

> When auto producers want to study world markets, they have access to data on all major world markets, not just on total output, but by sizes and models. All this information comes from easily available published data. Similarly when Xerox entered Latin America, they found useful proxy variables that helped them estimate the market for copying machines. The information came from their trade group, the Information Technology Industry Council (ITI), which had data on the international trade of its member companies.

Many firms will not be so fortunate as to find the data they want from their trade association. They must then look for international trade data on their product or a related product. The United Nations and the World Trade Organization are major sources of detailed trade data, and if the firm can find its product category, it will get an idea of both markets (importing countries) and competition (exporting countries). If the firm cannot find its product in the trade statistics, it would look for data on a product whose sales might correlate with its own. For example, the sales of copying machines might relate to the sales of computers, or the sales of automotive equipment to the number of motor vehicles in a given country. These two simple examples illustrate how the firm can look for proxy variables to evaluate global demand when no direct data is available for its own product. In looking for relevant proxy variables, the firm begins by analyzing its domestic market experience. The model of market demand based on domestic experience may not fit exactly in forecasting demand in foreign countries because of economic and cultural differences. However, it represents a good starting point for drawing on the information found in the varied sources of international data, such as the *United Nations' Statistical Yearbook*. The assessment of competition is discussed in the next section.

The Choice of Foreign Markets

U.S. firms generally do not make a major policy decision to go international; instead, they generally make decisions to enter specific foreign markets: Brazil, Canada, Germany, or western Europe. Ideally, however, the choice of foreign markets should be made like an investment decision—a selection of the best alternatives after considering all the relevant possibilities. The decision to enter foreign markets is, in fact, an investment decision, if not in plant facilities, at least in management time and other opportunities foregone. Let us approach it in that manner and consider ways to screen and rank foreign markets according to their attractiveness to the firm. A country will be attractive in relation to its market potential, competition, and political constraints.

Assessment of market potential in a country requires an analysis of local production and consumption plus imports and exports of the product in question. If hard data are not available, the researcher must construct a model using proxy variables for which data are available. For example, a firm that manufactures mouse pads and wrist rests found it easier to estimate sales potential by gathering information on computer sales, than attempting to collect data on computer accessories. Given the extensive amount of international economic and demographic data extant, the imaginative researcher should be able to come up with a model that provides useful estimates of market demand by country. It is not always an easy task, but it is feasible. We assume here that the firm is currently only a domestic marketer. If the firm has international experience, of course, it is in a much stronger position to evaluate foreign markets.

As part of the evaluation, a firm looks at *competition* and how it affects the attractiveness of a market. Even though a country has a large demand for a product, it may not be an attractive market if the competition has it locked up. For example, CPC International, which sells margarine in the U.S. market, does not sell it in the large European market because Unilever is so dominant in margarine products in Europe. One way to gain insight into the local competitive situation is to look at international trade data to find the major supplying countries. If a firm producing mechanotherapy apparatus (a type of medical equipment) wanted to know about its Japanese competition, for example, it could look in the *World Trade Annual* and find information as in Exhibit 4-3. This particular example shows the countries Japan is exporting to and the volume of their exports. Dividing the value by the weight would give a further idea as to the nature of the products by market—upper end versus lower end products. The same research and evaluation can be done for other exporting countries.

One must also ascertain local competition. If no industry or trade association data are available, the task is more difficult. One alternative is to visit the markets, but that can be expensive if one is considering markets in many countries. One information source is the commercial attaché in the U.S. embassies abroad. Their job is to promote U.S. firms' economic interests in the country. Another source is the American Chamber of Commerce, which can be found in many countries abroad. A final source is other companies with international experience. While competing firms would probably not be helpful, suppliers, including banks, or customers or other noncompeting firms may be willing to share valuable data. For example, when DuPont was considering building factories in Europe after having only export experience there, a management team visited Goodyear and other firms with European experience to learn about operating conditions. In international business quite a bit of this kind of exchange takes place.

The *political environment* is the third critical area in evaluating foreign markets. Countries that are attractive in terms of market potential and competition may become unattractive because of political considerations. Political instability in a country can spoil the market. Furthermore, hostile relations between the home and host country can make it a forbidden market. For example, U.S. firms may not deal with Cuba or Libya (see Chapter 2). Getting information on the political situation involves many of the same sources noted for the analysis of competition. Additionally, the U.S. State Department is an obvious source of expertise. Commercial services, the reliability of which can vary, also offer political evaluations of world markets.

EXHIBIT 4–3 *Exports by Commodity*

SITC* Number Export Destination	Quantity (metric tons)	Value (US $1,000s)
872.03 Mechano-Therapy Apparatus		
Japan . . . . . . .TOTAL	4,371	$157,104
South Africa	11	532
Egypt	1	188
Ethiopia	1	84
Cote d'Ivoire	3	221
Uganda	6	307
Tanzania	3	330
Zambia	1	172
Canada	35	838
United States	875	23,785
Argentina	1	53
Brazil	53	1,403
Chile	1	89
Ecuador	2	470
Cuba	2	122
Iran	4	195
Jordan	2	921
Kuwait	8	215
Oman	1	104
Saudi Arabia	34	831
United Arab Emirates	53	1,402
Bangladesh	5	73
Brunei	4	360
Sri Lanka	1	244
China	90	2,746
Hong Kong	217	6,313
Indonesia	11	619
Korea, Rep. (South)	140	7,430
Malaysia	14	634
Other Asia NES	1,988	78,220
Pakistan	3	73
Philippines	7	311
France	8	431
Germany	399	11,913
Italy	1	85

Source: *World Trade Annual, 1995* (New York: Walker & Company, 1997),
vol. IV, p. 557.
*Standard International Trade Classification (SITC)

The Choice of Entry into Foreign Markets

Many different approaches may be taken to enter foreign markets; the marketing implications vary significantly by entry method. We shall discuss entry methods in some depth in Chapter 6. Our concern here is with obtaining the information needed to choose the appropriate entry method: exporting, licensing, or local subsidiary. *Company* characteristics can greatly influence the choice of entry method, but we will consider here only the external market influences. *Size of market* is one factor and has already been discussed. *Trade barriers* such as tariffs and quotas could prevent exporting to a country. *Transportation* costs also affect the feasibility of exporting. Transportation companies are good information sources on this topic (shipping lines, airlines). The nature of *local competition* is another factor that might make one entry method more desirable than another. Evaluation of competition as a critical component of the process has already been discussed. Many *governments* have policies favoring one entry method over another, such as buying only goods produced in the country rather than imports. These factors were important considerations to foreign car manufacturers in their decision to move production to the United States. For American firms, these topics are rather easy to research as the U.S. Department of Commerce has good information on restrictions in foreign markets.

The Choice of Marketing Programs in Foreign Markets

Once the firm has become engaged in international business, the major part of its international marketing research will be concerned with the design of marketing programs for its foreign markets. These activities are similar to what is being done in the firm's domestic marketing research. The extent to which a firm can use its domestic techniques abroad provides obvious economies. Unfortunately, conditions in the foreign market frequently prevent the researcher from replicating what the firm does at home. These aspects will be discussed in the next section.

A firm must prepare marketing programs for two kinds of markets: those in which a firm is exporting to a distributor, and those in which a firm has a marketing subsidiary. Where the firm has a licensing arrangement, the licensee is the one primarily responsible for marketing. Where the firm has a marketing subsidiary, the marketing research task approximates what the firm does at home. For this reason we shall discuss the more difficult situation in distributor markets. It is also the most common international marketing situation. Because of the costs involved in setting up a marketing subsidiary, most firms have more distributor markets than they have markets with their own subsidiary.

Designing an appropriate marketing program requires information primarily in the areas of buyer behavior, competitive practice, distribution channels, and promotional media and practice. We saw in Chapter 3 the many differences in buyer behavior abroad. Because a firm usually can't afford to research buyer behavior in distributor markets, it must rely on other sources. Obvious candidates are the firm's distributor and advertising agency. They are located in the country and act as partners in the firm's marketing effort there. They indeed will be the major information source, not only on buyer behavior but also on competitive practice and the other variables.

A firm can, of course, expect limits to free information services. Both the distributor and the advertising agency have many clients, so the assistance they give to any one of them is dictated largely by the volume of business provided by that client. Furthermore, their primary business is the selling of marketing services, and the provision of information is incidental to that. The foreign exporter is also much more distant and unfamiliar than the local clients of the distributor or agency. For all these reasons, the exporting firm is somewhat handicapped in preparing marketing programs in distributor markets. Experience and personal visits are two ways firms increase their understanding and lessen their handicap.

PROBLEMS IN INTERNATIONAL MARKETING RESEARCH

Marketing research is a problematic activity even in the confines of a single country. It becomes much more so in a world economy that contains more than 200 nations and territories. We shall consider three types of problems in international marketing research not normally encountered in U.S. marketing research. Exhibit 4-4 provides an overview of these problems and the obstacles they present to the preparation of an international marketing research report. One type of problem arises from the number and size of the markets to be studied. A second problem area concerns the use of secondary data, and the third involves problems in gathering primary data. We shall now consider some approaches to dealing with these problems.

EXHIBIT 4-4   *The Tortuous Path of International Marketing Research*

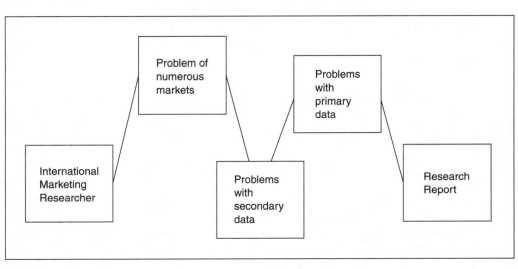

Number and Size of Markets

Dealing with larger numbers usually means economies of scale. This notion holds true if the units are homogeneous. In world markets, however, each is unique in varying degrees in its buyer behavior and data availability. Their uniqueness means diseconomies of scale and a new learning curve for the researcher. Many firms need to consider more than 100 countries in their international marketing. The challenge is to find an effective and economical way to meet that need. Part of the problem arises because many foreign markets are small in terms of population and income, as we saw in Chapter 2. Indeed, for the U.S. firm, nearly all foreign markets are smaller than the home market. Marketing research costs money, and the firm cannot afford to pay more for research than the value of the information to be obtained from it. The value of the information is less in small markets, and therefore less research can be profitably undertaken there. This restriction is especially true if the research is based on a sampling procedure. Sample size is not dependent on the size of the universe. Thus, a probability sample in Uruguay would need the same sample size as one in the giant U.S. economy if the standard deviation in the two populations is the same.

Problems with Secondary Data

Printed and electronically available publications that are provided by governments, trade associations, the UN, and other organizations account for much of the secondary data available to market researchers. A problem with international secondary data is *scarcity;* many countries simply do not have research data available. The United States is unmatched for the wealth of economic and demographic data available, though the other industrialized countries generally do a good job too. This abundance is due in part to efforts of the U.S. government as the world's largest information gathering agency. The availability of secondary data in a country corresponds roughly to its level of economic development.

> Bolivia hasn't had a census since 1950 and Congo since 1958. The situation in former communist countries is ambiguous. In 1980, when China was opening up to dealings with western firms, some of the first figures on the Chinese economy were made publicly available. Officials admitted that some of the figures were drawn from CIA studies. China is probably not typical, but it does indicate some of the problems with secondary data. China's first industrial census was conducted in 1986.

Reliability is another problem with secondary data. Governments are the major data gatherers, and governments are concerned about their image. They may underreport negative items such as illiteracy or disease and overreport favorable items such as industrial production. National data can also be used for political purposes, to influence the amount of assistance from the World Bank or a donor country. In other words, some countries tell it as it is; others tell it as they would like it to appear. In the latter case, reliability suffers. Even apart from political or image considerations, data reliability varies internationally according to the nation's skill and sophistication in data gathering. Just as market research can be difficult for the firm, so information gathering is difficult for governments. Many countries have both limited resources and a shortage of skilled personnel for gathering data on their economies. If, with all of its resources and experience, the United States has problems administering the census or defining "generally accepted accounting principles," imagine the situation in African or Latin American countries.

The analysis of international secondary data is further complicated by issues of *comparability.* If the firm is to evaluate foreign countries and rank them according to their attractiveness as markets, it must have data that can be compared. Even where data are available and reliable, they may not be comparable. Items of interest to the researcher will often be defined differently from country to country. Let's say one is interested in truck markets around the world. Truck statistics might be found in their pure form as a separate data classification, or they might include vans, or they may be in a category called "commercial vehicles," which includes taxis, buses, and perhaps tractors. Identifying and comparing a product market in countries using differing definitions and classifications can be difficult.

The same difficulty may occur regardless of the aspect of interest in a particular market or marketing environment. Occasionally different weights and measures are used—long ton and metric ton, for example. About the only unambiguous figure is the population of the country, and as noted, this figure is often a guesstimate. If one is studying channels of distribution, one will find differing definitions of wholesalers, retailers, and supermarkets. In the case of television markets, Germany reports TV set purchases under the heading "recreation and entertainment," while in the United States the category is "furniture, furnishings, and household equipment." In this case, three categories of data are not comparable: the TV set market, the recreation and entertainment market, and the furniture, furnishings and household equipment market.

ESOMAR (the European Society for Opinion and Marketing Research) has a working paper on "Harmonization of Demographics." ESOMAR feels that if Europe is indeed going to be a single market, then conducting marketwide research should be possible there, rather than having to do separate and different country studies in each market. To facilitate this objective, demographic definitions have to be harmonized so that terms such as "housewife," "professional," and "middle class" mean the same everywhere. The age brackets of the life cycle should likewise be the same in each member country.

A final aspect of comparability is the timeliness of data. Data that are otherwise good and reliable may have been gathered at different times, in extreme cases perhaps five or ten years apart. One must try to evaluate the data at some common base year.

Problems in Obtaining Primary Data

Because secondary data pose problems in international marketing research and because they are, almost by definition, not specific to the firm's needs, primary data gathering will often be necessary. A variety of problems can arise in conducting primary research abroad. One is the *economic problem* that was discussed previously, that is, the fact that reliable data may be as expensive to get in a small market as in a big market, given the requirements of probability sampling. Because the value of the information is not as great in a small market, the firm may not be able to afford primary research in small countries. Even where primary data gathering is economically feasible, the researcher must be prepared for other kinds of problems.

Response Problems

Response problems come in different forms because people's response behavior is culturally conditioned. In some Far East countries, such as Japan, a tradition of courtesy makes for cooperative respondents, but they say things that will please the interviewer, even if the statements don't provide an accurate picture of the subject being investigated. In Muslim countries, women are not allowed to talk to a male interviewer, and women are not allowed to be interviewers. In many countries, industrial market research is hampered by the reluctance of potential respondents. The reticence of business respondents stems in part from a desire for competitive secrecy. Frequently, however, a greater reason for mistrust of those calling themselves market researchers is the fear that the interviewer is really a government tax agent. Tax evasion is a way of life in some countries, and respondents want nothing to do with any questions about their economic activities.

Language and Translation

Language and translation problems are common in international marketing research. Each foreign market will probably have a language different from that of the international marketer, and some will have several languages. Frequently, the firm will want to replicate in foreign markets a successful domestic market research project. This desire is logical, but extreme care is necessary for successful implementation. The research instrument cannot merely be translated into the foreign language. If more than factual data is desired, such as information about attitudes or motivation, it is imperative that the ideas and concepts be translated, not just the words. That is to say, the cultural barrier must be crossed as well as the language barrier. A literal translation won't necessarily achieve that objective.

Back translation, where material is translated into the foreign language, then back to the original language is one technique used to reduce interpretation problems. Comparing the first and the final versions can be used to determine if the intended message is received. Another method, in which two versions of the translated material are prepared by different translators and then compared for inconsistencies is called parallel translation.

Multilingual societies compound the language problem. A country that is otherwise large enough to warrant an economic research project may be fragmented by several languages. In this situation one might be tempted to use the official language, say, French or English, only to find that only a small part of the population speaks that language. In many countries, *lingua francas* or language bridges are used for communication between different language groups. A lingua franca is usually the language of one major group that is used as the communications medium between a number of groups speaking different languages. For example, Swahili plays this role in several African nations, as does Hindi in India. These lingua francas are second languages for most of the users, and they often do not communicate the true meaning, which is necessary in consumer research.

Literacy and Education

Low levels of literacy and education are barriers to market research. Where illiteracy prevails, written questionnaires are useless. Even when a country has a reasonable level of literacy, if literacy is accompanied by a generally low level of education, communications problems will still persist. Respondents may answer according to their understanding of the question, but their interpretation may be a misunderstanding of the question's true meaning. The problem in this case does not lie with the respondent, but in the design of the research.

Inadequate Infrastructure

Inadequate infrastructure for marketing research is perhaps the most serious problem of all. *Telephone* surveys, for example, would not be feasible in countries where only a small portion of urban dwellers have phones. The problem is exacerbated in areas that have no telephone books, as in such major cities as Cairo and Tehran. Mail surveys require both literacy and reliable *postal service,* and countries that are weak in one of these areas tend to be weak in the other also. However, even some developed countries such as Italy are notorious for their unreliable mail delivery.

BOX 4-2   *Gold Key Service Offers Custom Export Market Assistance*

The Gold Key Service is part of the U.S. government's efforts to promote U.S. exports and, thereby, create jobs. Rather than conduct the research themselves, U.S. firms can turn to the Department of Commerce. Benefits include:

- Reduction of time and money expenditures. The U.S. Commercial Service will screen markets and find the best contracts.
- Arrangements to meet people who suit the firm's specific requirements. Whether the exporter is looking for company representatives, distributors, government officials, or licensing or joint venture partners, the Gold Key Service will match the right people to the company's needs.
- Less time and expense spent on logistics. Experienced staff will hire interpreters, help with travel and accommodations, provide clerical support, screen business candidates, and make appointments.
- Customized market and industry briefings. Commercial Service personnel provide reports, and brief company representatives prior to business meetings. They also arrange a debriefing with trade specialists afterwards.
- Continued counseling and export promotion. Upon returning to the United States, the company is afforded assistance through local Export Assistance Centers.

The Gold Key Service is available in more than 70 of the world's best U.S. export markets, at fees ranging from $150 to $600. Exporters can avail themselves of this service by contacting one of the Department of Commerce's district offices throughout the country, or the commercial service officers who are attached to U.S. embassies around the world.

The International Trade Administration, which is also a part of the U.S. Department of Commerce, provides a number of other programs and forms of assistance to U.S. firms. They include market research information (National Trade Data Bank and Industry Sector Analysis), identification of export prospects (Trade Opportunities Program and Agent/Distributor Service), and product and service promotion in foreign countries (Matchmaker Trade Delegations and International Buyer Program).

Source: The Commercial Service, U.S. Department of Commerce, <http://www.ita.doc.gov/uscs/uscsgold.html> and <http://www.ita.doc.gov/uscs/uscshelp.html>

Other necessary inputs for conducting research are *marketing research organizations* and people who are trained to work in this area. The major industrial nations generally foster good facilities for market research, including such groups as A. C. Nielsen. In formerly communist countries and the poorer developing nations, marketing research organizations are weak or nonexistent. Nonetheless, a number of developing countries have surprisingly good capabilities for marketing research, sometimes in connection with big U.S. international advertising agencies. J. Walter Thompson (Hindustan Thompson, Bombay) provides service in India, for example, but other agencies can be found there as well. Perhaps the best proxy variable to indicate a country's marketing research capability would be its per capita advertising expenditure.

SPECIAL APPROACHES IN INTERNATIONAL MARKETING RESEARCH

Because of the problems of international marketing research that we have discussed, researchers have developed special approaches to assist them in learning about foreign markets. One approach is to look for help from home, to get your domestic advertising agency or marketing research firm to establish offices abroad. Such approaches are common in international business. Indeed, the major force behind the international spread of U.S. service organizations (banks, advertising agencies, etc.) is their desire to keep up with their clients who are taking their businesses international. Because of these pressures, the developing countries with the best services are those with the largest foreign business presence.

Learn by Doing

In many markets, firms find that the difficulties of primary marketing research are so great that it is not economically feasible to do it, given the size of the market. But another way of learning about the market is to test it by exports. Rather than surveying buyers about their attitudes toward the firm and its products, the firm can get actual market experience by exporting to the country. Exporting can be a low-cost and short-term method for the firm to enter a foreign market. After a year or two of export experience, the firm will know much more about actual market behavior than could be learned from a preliminary market study. If the market proves difficult or unprofitable, the firm can withdraw without major losses. However, if the market proves particularly attractive, the firm might consider a heavier commitment in the country. In either case, the firm has actual experience on which to base its decision rather than just market research data.

International Trade Fairs

Each year more than 1,500 trade fairs take place in countries around the world. A trade fair covering a firm's product line and geographic interests can be a valuable opportunity for gaining marketing intelligence. At the fair, the firm will encounter potential customers and can check their reaction to its offerings. Competitors' products and customer reaction to them can also be noted. Potential distributors or agents are also likely to be at the fair. All in all, trade fairs can be an efficient investment in market research because so many of the relevant actors are gathered together at one time and place.

Improvisation

Improvisation can scarcely be called a technique. Yet it is the best term to describe the ad hoc ingenuity employed by international marketing researchers in trying to overcome the kinds of problems we have discussed. The actual characteristics of improvisation can't be easily described because they are idiosyncratic to the firm and the foreign market situation. However, improvisation involves such activities as finding proxy variables when data are not available for the primary variables, or finding ways to get reaction to a proposed new product when it isn't possible to do conventional surveys or market tests. As noted earlier, John Kracmar of Singer wrote a book on how to deal with problems of marketing research in the developing countries. All market research can be likened to detective work, but whereas the domestic researcher might be likened to a city detective, the international researcher would be more like an agent for the CIA, or perhaps James Bond, though a bit less glamorous.

Comparative Analysis

Classification is the beginning of science, and comparative analysis in international marketing is an attempt by the firm to identify meaningful classifications of world markets. To help our understanding, we can group the countries of the world in several different ways. For example, we speak of North versus South; the first, second, and third worlds; the six continents; or Rostow's division of the world into five stages of economic development. Each of these classifications offers insights into some aspect of the political or economic situation of the countries of the world. Classifications improve our understanding because they are a form of generalization that provides structure to a mass of data.

The international marketer can't always use existing classifications of the countries of the world because they were not developed for the firm's needs. In other cases, they can be a useful starting point. For example, a food company executive told us that he found Rostow's classification approach useful for his analysis of foreign markets. In general, however, the international researcher must develop country categories that are appropriate to the firm's specific situation, because no general marketing classification is suitable for all firms. Just as the geographer, political analyst, and the economist have various ways of grouping countries, so would companies that manufacture chemicals, computers, and cosmetics have different country classifications, just as they have different ways of segmenting their domestic markets.

Preparing a comparative analysis for international marketing is not an esoteric activity. As we said, it is a form of generalization, something we do all the time. The parallel in domestic marketing is the way the firm identifies market segments. The major difference, of course, is that market segments are based on individual *consumer* characteristics, whereas country classifications are based on characteristics of entire *nations*. The researcher needs to identify the country's economic, demographic, and other dimensions that affect a firm's marketing there.

For the firm without any international experience, the identification of the relevant variables for comparative analysis would start with an assessment or model of how the firm relates to its environment in the home market. Firms already selling abroad can more easily identify the characteristics of foreign markets that correlate with the firm's marketing success. One statistical technique for achieving this objective is cluster analysis, a method of grouping like things together. Of course, the likeness is in the eye of the beholder, and the grouping of like countries for CPC International, which has used this kind of analysis, is different from the grouping for Pfizer, which has also used country groupings. While CPC's important variables would include items such as per capita income and food habits, a pharmaceutical marketer such as Pfizer would consider variables that include the existence of a national health service in a country and the number of hospitals and doctors.

The way in which firms can prepare such comparative analyses is a matter of statistical technique and is better discussed elsewhere. All we are suggesting here is that comparative analysis and country groupings can be important aids in understanding foreign markets and planning marketing strategy there. For this reason, many consumer and industrial goods firms use this approach, rather than grouping markets by geographic region. Cluster analysis has several advantages. One is *economy*. If a firm can accurately and meaningfully group world markets into a small number of categories, market analysis becomes easier and more efficient than when dealing with 100–150 individual countries as unique entities. The countries in a group are treated in a similar manner just as millions of customers in a market segment are treated similarly in the firm's domestic marketing.

Country groupings are effective to the degree that they accurately reflect the similarity of marketing characteristics. Inappropriate groupings lead to misunderstanding and poor decisions. If the comparisons are well done, however, not only are they efficient, but they also *increase our understanding* of the phenomena we are analyzing. In other words, comparative analysis can provide economy and efficiency in the study of foreign markets.

Other advantages can be derived from comparative analysis of country groupings. One is in dealing with countries with *missing data.* In any grouping of countries, some will undoubtedly lack data on key variables. If these countries are part of a group that is homogeneous in terms of other variables important to the firm, the researcher can reasonably assume that the values for the missing data are similar to those available for other countries in the same group. While this assumption will not always be accurate, it is a feasible and reasonable approach to take with such data gaps.

Another advantage of comparative analysis comes when dealing with the *expense* of trying to do market research in many small markets. If the firm has grouped its world markets in meaningful categories, it can conduct research in one or a few countries in a grouping and extrapolate the results to the other countries in the group. While this approach must be used carefully, it has the same advantages and limitations of any quota or stratified sampling technique. It is better than the alternatives of conducting no research at all or doing high-cost research in a large number of smaller countries.

INFORMATION SOURCES

Many firms remain purely domestic marketers even though market opportunities are available abroad. They are usually unaware of these foreign opportunities and feel learning about them is too difficult and expensive. Because we have emphasized the problems of international marketing research, we must take some space to emphasize the opposite point: it is possible to do rather extensive low-cost international marketing research within the United States because of the abundance of information sources in the country. We shall furnish only a broad overview of information sources. As mentioned, these sources provide this information in printed form as well as electronic media. Some information can be custom-ordered to meet the needs of the researcher better. For example, the World Bank provides a summary of its world tables in print, has a website with selected data available on the Internet free of charge, and sells a compact disc with about 500 variables on more than 150 countries, which covers a 35-year period. The following list describes some resources used in international marketing research.

1. The U.S. government is the world's largest information service. Fortunately, one part of its information deals with markets and marketing conditions abroad, and it is meant to help U.S. firms in their international marketing efforts. The information is either free or highly subsidized and therefore provides a valuable resource for the firm looking at world markets. The Department of Commerce is the major source of this information, and it can be accessed conveniently at its field offices in major cities across the country as well as on the Internet.

2. All major foreign governments have embassies and/or consulates in this country, which are useful sources of information about their home markets. They vary in the amount of data they can provide, and a political bias may skew the data, so usefulness of data varies by country.

3. International organizations such as the World Bank (IBRD), the International Monetary Fund, the Organization for Economic Cooperation and Development (OECD), and various United Nations organizations all have extensive international data, much of which is of interest and available to international marketers in some form and usually at moderate cost.

4. Various industry associations, such as in automobiles or chemicals, gather international as well as national data for their members. Examples were cited earlier. Additionally business groups include members from a wide range of industries, such as the Chamber of Commerce, the Directory of Associations (available from the American Society of Association Executives), the Federation of International Trade Associations (FITA), and the World Trade Centers Association. All these groups can provide assistance for their members in answering a variety of international business questions.

5. Service organizations such as major accounting firms, advertising agencies, and banks are involved in international business, and they can be especially helpful to their client companies who are contemplating or

engaged in international marketing. Because of the relationship between client and the service provider much of the information is available free. International airlines and shipping companies are also helpful
even with questions that go beyond physical distribution.

6. Information service organizations make their living by selling information rather than by providing it free. Consulting firms would be included
here as well as such established services as Business International and
Economist Intelligence Unit. Some of these organizations are very good
at their job but tend to be proportionately more expensive.

7. Noncompeting companies, such as suppliers or customers who have
international experience, are often able and willing to provide helpful
information concerning foreign markets. Contacts can be made with
these firms through common membership in business groups and the
foreign trade clubs found in many U.S. cities.

8. Most of the organizations cited here have published information in various forms. A great number of specialized publications also deal with
many of the issues and kinds of information pertinent to international
marketing. Among this diverse collection of information sources are the
National Trade and Professional Associations of the U.S., the *Exporter's
Encyclopedia*, and countless directories of manufacturers, importers,
and other kinds of businesses in world markets.

SUCCESS AND FAILURE IN INTERNATIONAL MARKETING RESEARCH

Ford Motor Co. is a successful international marketer who sometimes depends on foreign earnings to offset a bad year in the U.S. market. But just
as every product or idea is not a winner at home, occasional reverses
abroad can be related to the results of marketing research.

Failure In the 1970s, Ford introduced the Fiera into Thailand. Fiera was a
low-cost utilitarian vehicle, specially designed to be the "Model T for Asia."
It was a top seller in the Philippines, but it failed in Thailand. The primary
reason was poor marketing research.

- Ford was unable to gauge the tastes and preferences of Thai consumers
  who were attracted to the image and performance of Japanese cars.
- Ford overestimated the favorable impact of Fiera's lower price because
  cars were usually bought on installment plans.

- The load placed on vehicles in Thailand frequently exceeds design capacity as much as two or three times, causing frequent breakdowns in the Fiera. A sturdier model was introduced too late.
- Ford had expected the Thai government to impose a ban on imports, but it never did, forcing Ford to cover the expense of its decision to produce the Fiera locally.

Success Four years before Fiesta was launched, Ford began to define the concept through market research. Studies showed what consumers wanted in terms of styling and performance, durability, front-wheel drive, and so forth. Internal and external design were consumer tested. Consumer interviews were conducted in the five major market countries to choose a name. Similar research was done to develop both advertising *themes*—safety, durability, economy—and advertising *campaigns*. The introduction was successful; in three of the five major markets, Ford's market share increased significantly.

SUMMARY

Marketing research is a complicated and technical subject to which business schools often devote an entire course. This chapter allows only enough space to note some of the distinctive features of international marketing research, such as its broad scope and cross-cultural complications. When a firm begins marketing internationally, it usually draws on the marketing research techniques and expertise it has developed domestically. This seemingly obvious approach often has its limitations. We have indicated a few of the problems that may accompany attempts to replicate domestic marketing research in foreign countries. We have also suggested some special approaches for dealing with the problems of conducting international marketing research. The purpose of conducting marketing research is to obtain information to help in making marketing decisions. We now turn to the international marketing decisions that depend upon the information gathered in research in order to answer the questions of what product? what price? what promotion? and what distribution? We shall begin with product policy in international marketing.

QUESTIONS

1. Show how the task of international marketing research is more comprehensive than that of domestic marketing research.

2. Identify the different types of decisions for which international marketing research is needed.
3. What kinds of information are needed to enable firms to choose foreign markets?
4. Discuss some of the problems encountered in researching foreign markets.
5. Discuss the special problems in using secondary data in international marketing research.
6. How can firms "gather information" in lieu of formal market research in foreign markets?
7. Show how comparative analysis can help firms better understand foreign markets.
8. Identify the major kinds of information sources available for international marketing research.

FURTHER READING

1. Cateora, Philip R. and John L. Graham, *International Marketing,* 10th ed. (Boston, MA: Irwin/McGraw-Hill, 1999), Chapter 8.
2. Douglas, Susan P. and Samuel Craig, *International Marketing Research: Concepts & Methods* (Chichester, England: John Wiley & Sons, 1999).
3. Jain, Subhash C., *International Marketing Management,* 5th ed. (Cincinnati: South-Western College Publishing, 1996), Chapter 10.
4. Koh, Anthony C., "International Marketing Research by U.S. Export Firms," *Journal of Global Marketing* vol. 4, no. 3 (1991), pp. 7–25.
5. Kracmar, John Z., *Marketing Research in the Developing Countries: A Handbook* (New York: Praeger, 1971).
6. Liander, Bertil, Vern Terpstra, M. Y. Yoshino, and Aziz A. Sherbini, *Comparative Analysis for International Marketing* (Boston: Allyn and Bacon, 1967).
7. Russow, Lloyd C. and Sam C. Okorcafo, "On the Way toward Developing a Global Screening Model," *International Marketing Review* vol. 13, no. 1 (1996), pp. 46–64.

NOTE: Basic marketing texts have one or more chapters that cover marketing research.

Product Strategies for World Markets

CHOOSING PRODUCTS FOR WORLD MARKETS

The most fundamental questions a firm can ask itself are What business are we in? and What business should we be in? The answers to those questions will determine the products and services the firm offers to the market. The questions are fundamental because if the firm chooses the wrong business to be in, it will be short-lived. Today, divestment seems to be as popular an activity as diversification was two decades ago; we see many diversified firms shedding businesses they found attractive only a short time ago. In international marketing, the issue of which business to be in is just as critical as in domestic marketing. It is a more complicated issue, however, because the firm must decide which business to be in within each of its foreign markets. The firm may not be in completely different businesses in each foreign market, but its business profile in each country will be unique.

The firm's business in a foreign market will be defined largely, but not entirely, by the products it sells there. For example, an advertising agency would probably be in the advertising business in its foreign markets, but its involvement there could range from a wholly owned full service agency

BOX 5-1   *Colgate-Palmolive Company's Global Product Strategies*

Colgate-Palmolive products are sold in more than 200 countries. Sales in 1997 exceeded $9 billion, nearly one-third of which came from products introduced since 1992. North America and Europe each accounted for 22 percent of sales, Latin America for 26 percent, and Asia and Africa together for 19 percent of sales. Gross income increased more than 25 percent over the last five years, and net income increased 17 percent in 1997 alone.

The growth in sales and market leadership are attributed to powerful global brands. Mennen, Ajax, Hill's Science Diet, and the full lines of Colgate toothpaste and Palmolive soap are recognized around the world. Fabuloso and Fête des Fleurs are big soap brands outside the United States.

Each year Colgate surveys more than 500,000 consumers in 30 countries to keep ahead of changing needs, habits, and usage patterns. In 1997, the company created separate divisions for high-growth markets and for developed markets. Its new product innovation center in Mexico, designed to keep the company in close contact with its Latin American consumers, is part of a trend to develop area-specific centers worldwide.

Products designed in one country must often be adapted for other markets. Names are changed to be more meaningful in the local language; product fragrances are different in type and amount (Europeans like long-lasting fragrances); ingredients are removed or added (Palmolive Natural hair products sold in Poland are herbal and vitamin-enriched). Sometimes products—such as Ajax Expel, a cleanser that also repels insects (popular in Portugal, Spain and Italy)—are developed for specific markets. On the other hand, Total toothpaste is designed to meet multiple consumer needs in a broad market segment and is virtually identical in the 104 countries in which it is sold.

Rueben Mark, chairman and CEO, said, "We try to live up to our vision of becoming the best *truly global consumer products company.*" A strong global product strategy is an essential ingredient to the company's continued success.

Source: Colgate-Palmolive Company 1997 Annual Report and Management Letter <http://www.colgate.com>.

to various kinds of lesser commitments to as little as a cooperative arrangement with a national agency. An automobile manufacturer would probably be in the automobile business in its foreign markets, but its involvement could range from wholly owned manufacturing and marketing facilities to assembly plants to company marketing subsidiaries to exports sold to independent national distributors. This level of involvement aspect of the firm's business abroad will be discussed in Chapter 6. Here we shall look at the firm's business abroad as defined by the products it sells there.

EXHIBIT 5-1   *The Total Product*

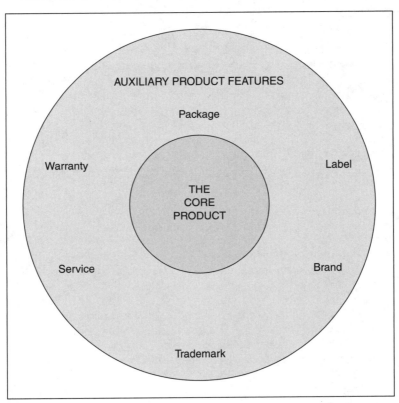

AUXILIARY PRODUCT FEATURES

Package

Warranty

THE
CORE
PRODUCT

Label

Service

Brand

Trademark

We shall start with the individual product, looking first at its physical characteristics and then at auxiliary product features, such as packaging, brand, and warranty. Exhibit 5-1 illustrates how the total product is composed of the core product plus the auxiliary product features.

THE CORE PRODUCT

We define product as everything the consumer receives when making the purchase: the actual physical product, the package, brand, post sale service, and whatever the psychological return associated with all its characteristics. We begin our discussion with the actual physical product or what can be called the core product for foreign markets. The appropriate question here is, What product will best achieve our goals in world mar-

kets? The question is more often stated as: Can we sell our domestic product abroad? Because the question is typically in the latter form, some
merit is found in considering the feasibility of making a firm's standard
domestic product also serve as its standard world product.

The Domestic Product as World Product

Firms have many reasons for wanting to sell their domestic product un-
changed to foreign markets. The obvious reason is that it is the easiest thing
to do. Another reason is the economies that might be realized. Use of the same
raw materials, equipment, and processes leads to *manufacturing economies*
of scale that could be lost if the firm had to change the standard product. The
more similar the firm's product is from country to country, the more alike the
marketing and service requirements will be, giving rise to *marketing economies.* Another kind of economy arises from the savings the firm realizes by
not having to conduct *market and product* research for foreign markets. If, for
example, the firm chose not to sell its standard domestic product abroad, it
would need to conduct market research to determine what to sell and then engage in product development to come up with the right new product.

Other conditions favor the sale of the standard domestic product
abroad. One is the existence of *international customers.* For example,
an automobile manufacturer with plants in Brazil, Mexico, and France
doesn't want three different kinds of bearings from Timken; it wants uniform bearings for all plants. The tourist visiting a number of countries buying such things as disposable razors, Coca-Cola, or Kodak film expects a
uniform product from country to country. The existence of a *national image* for certain products also favors the sale of the standard domestic product. In some countries, for example, U.S. chewing gum, jeans, and
cigarettes have a favorable image, and consumers prefer the U.S. product.

Where conditions are favorable for extending the domestic product
abroad, they are reinforced by the international *product life cycle.* The
product life cycle says that after being introduced, products experience a
period of rapid growth followed by a period of maturity and, eventually,
decline. This phenomenon can be observed for most products in most
countries. The life cycle of a specific product, however, varies from country to country like other cultural phenomena. The United States is one of
the more affluent economies in the world, and products near the end of
their life cycle here may be at the introductory or growth stage of their
life cycle in many foreign markets. This situation provides the firm an

excellent opportunity to extend sales of such a product by offering it in those foreign markets.

> Gillette introduced many different kinds of disposable razors and razor blades during the past 20 years. Some of the newest types aren't even sold in some of the less-developed countries. In contrast, the double-edged stainless steel blade, which is in the decline stage of its life cycle in the United States, is the leading seller in some African, Asian, and Latin American markets.

Localized versus International Products

In a surprising number of cases the standard domestic product is sold in foreign markets. Perrier, Coca-Cola, Kellogg's Corn Flakes, and Kodak film are examples. In many more cases, however, some adaptation of the product is necessary, not just for foreign markets, but for *individual* foreign markets. Firms prefer to sell a uniform product in all countries, so we must ascertain what factors induce them to undertake the more costly course of adapting their products. These factors fall into two categories: mandatory adaptation and discretionary adaptation.

Mandatory Adaptation

Mandatory adaptation involves those situations in which the firm adapts its products because some aspect of the foreign market requires it to do so. If the firm wants to be in the market, it has no choice but to modify its product. One such factor for U.S. firms is the *metric system* used in almost every other country. Any U.S. product sold abroad for which measurement is an important variable must be produced or labeled according to metric standards. This requirement covers a great variety of products ranging from Armstrong ceilings and floors to the nuts and bolts in machinery to pharmaceutical measures. Because of the increasing U.S. economic interdependence with the rest of the world, stated national policy encourages metric compliance. Understandably, multinational firms are leading the way because of their dependence on world markets and the need to rationalize production in different countries. *Differing electrical systems* are another factor. Most consumer and industrial products run by electricity are sensitive to the cycles and voltage of the electrical power supply. Try, for example, to plug in a U.S. CD player in a Brussels apartment and watch what happens! Exhibit 5-2 lists some of the variation in electrical power systems. Note that some countries have two different systems.

EXHIBIT 5-2   *Electrical Power Differences*

Country	Hertz (cycles)	Volts
Algeria	50	127/220
Bolivia	50	220/230
	50	115 (La Paz & Viacha)
Japan	50	100 (Eastern Japan)
	60	100 (Western Japan)
Kenya	50	240
Mexico	60	127
Namibia	50	220
	50	230 (Keetmanshoop)
United States	60	120

Source: <http://www.kropla.com/electric2.htm>

The major foreign market factor forcing product adaptation on the firm is, of course, *government*. In the United States we have the Food and Drug Administration, the Environmental Protection Agency, and the Occupational Safety and Health Administration, all of which have a voice in the regulation of products. Other industrialized countries have counterpart organizations to protect their consumers. The interesting aspect in this matter is that, though the human body is biologically and physiologically the same in every country, each country has different product requirements to protect its citizens. The effect of these requirements discourages imported products, and therefore their net result provides as much protection to the producers within the country as to its consumers. For that reason government regulations are often called *nontariff barriers* to trade. Developing countries require less in the area of consumer protection and product regulation. The irony of the situation, however, is that with lower levels of literacy, education, and buying experience, the consumers in developing countries need more rather than less protection.

Governments everywhere have a pervasive role in product regulation. In the United States some of the more publicized cases have been emission standards, mileage requirements, bumper strength, and air bags in automobiles; flammable nightwear; red dye and sweeteners in food; and phosphates in detergent. The automotive industry is one of the most highly controlled. Developed countries tend to regulate the same things the U.S. government regulates, such as safety and emissions, but they have different specifications in these areas, sometimes more strict than

U.S. standards. In motor vehicle noise standards, for example, the Europeans will allow no more than 82 decibels as measured 25 feet from the driving lane, whereas the U.S. requirement is 84 decibels measured 50 feet from the driving lane.

Developing countries often have even more extreme product requirements but of a different kind. The Andean Common Market (ANCOM) countries decided they could not afford the proliferation of motor vehicle models resulting from letting each foreign producer do as it pleased. They specified the characteristics of a limited number of models of cars and trucks that they would allow and then asked foreign producers to bid for the right to make those models in the Andean countries. General Motors, Ford, and many other producers entered the bidding.

The automobile, as a visible consumer item, often faces highly publicized regulations. Government regulation hits more mundane products as well. As noted earlier, German noise requirements kept British lawn mowers off German lawns, and British producers felt that the costs of adaptation were too high. Food processing is another highly regulated industry. Nations tend to differ in the allowable percentages of sugar and fruit in a jar of jam, the amount of water in canned vegetables, the kind and amount of preservatives in cereals and other packaged foods, and so on for almost every processed food product. It would be tedious rather than instructive to catalog the varieties of government regulation across industries. Suffice it to say that governmental product specification is a fact of life in marketing today. International marketers cannot expect less regulation. They can only work for the establishment of international standards that would lessen the diseconomies of present approaches.

> One of the more exotic and extreme examples of government product regulation occurred in Singapore. In 1992, Singapore banned the import, manufacture, or sale of chewing gum. The Environmental Ministry, in announcing the ban, cited incidents in which pranksters put wads of gum on subway doors preventing their closing, as well as the frequent deposit of gum on subway seats. Now chewing gum importers face a fine of 10,000 Singapore dollars and a year in jail. Retailers who handle bootleg gum can be fined 2,000 Singapore dollars.

Discretionary Adaptation

Discretionary product adaptation is more interesting than mandatory adaptation because here the firm has more control of its fate. The firm alone decides whether to modify its products and how to modify them. This kind of product modification is also more problematic because no guidelines specify how the product should be modified. It is the opposite of mandatory adaptation where technical or government requirements are unambiguous. Let us consider some of the market factors that might encourage firms to adapt their products.

One pressure for adaptation is the *different levels of income* in foreign markets. Consumers at similar levels of affluence are able to afford similar products, whether it be a Rolls Royce, a color TV, air travel, or convenience foods. Several different levels of income in the world, however, mean that not all consumers can afford to purchase the same goods. As a general rule, in low-income countries a cheaper, stripped-down version will find a market different to the firm's home market, which is the case across most product categories. The sewing machines Singer sells in Africa are simple, basic, inexpensive, and hand-powered. General Motors does not sell its standard Cadillac in poor countries, nor even its standard Chevrolet. It developed a basic transportation vehicle (BTV) for such markets. In the industrial goods field, General Electric was losing business in developing countries for its standard steam-generating power systems because its bids were too high. It developed a stripped-down version costing hundreds of thousands of dollars less and began to win lucrative contracts. This process of developing simpler products is sometimes called *reverse engineering* or *inventing backward.*

Differing consumer tastes are an important factor inducing product modifications by international marketers. We saw earlier how Campbell had trouble trying to sell U.S. formula soups in Europe. After some years of red ink, Campbell was induced to adapt to European soup tastes and came out with an Italian tomato soup, a British tomato soup, and so on. Campbell is now making profits in Europe.

> Philip Morris advertises its U.S. cigarette brands heavily in domestic media. Because these media spill over into Canada, Philip Morris felt it had a natural advantage in selling its U.S. brands there. It soon discovered, however, that Canadian preferences were for a different blend of tobaccos, emphasizing Virginia tobacco as in the English cigarettes to which Canadians were accustomed.
>
> Heublein's big international business is its Kentucky Fried Chicken franchises. When the company opened its first outlets in Israel, it authorized a rare product modification. Its Israeli outlets serve kosher chicken, the first for the company. Interestingly, the franchisee for these outlets is a New York lawyer.

These few incidents merely confirm that tastes are subjective and, being culturally determined, vary from country to country. For a marketing-oriented firm, the lesson is obvious. In questions of taste and fashion in product design, it behooves the firm when in Rome to become more like the Romans. Nestlé illustrates the wisdom of this strategy with their Nescafé brand of coffee, which has become the world's leader in instant coffee. They have dozens of blends of Nescafé around the world. The local formulations were determined according to taste tests in different national markets.

> When Nabisco went to Japan, consumers there found the Oreos too sweet, so the amount of sugar was reduced to give them a more bitter taste. Some consumers still found them too sweet, so Nabisco added a modified Oreo product—without the cream.

Another factor that may encourage firms to modify their products is *the level of education and technical sophistication* in foreign markets. Not only do consumers in affluent countries average about 10 years of formal education, they have also grown up living and learning in economies that are advanced commercially, industrially, and scientifically. In countries where children learn to use computers when they are quite young, few limits restrict the complexity and sophistication of products that can be offered to consumers or to industry. Many countries of the world are at much lower levels of education and technical sophistication. There the average household does not have a car or a collection of electrical or electronic gadgets. In these countries consumers can't use products with the same degree of complexity that U.S. consumers can handle. For this reason, General Motors' basic transportation vehicle was designed not just to be inexpensive, but also simple to operate and easy to maintain. By the same token, workers in these countries can't handle complex and technically sensitive machines, so industrial marketers are as much affected as consumer marketers.

> In one African nation, farmers had been spraying their crops with a simple but primitive duster. A U.S. firm came in with a new duster, still hand-operated but much quicker and more efficient for the task. After demonstrations proved the superiority of the new duster, it was adopted. After a few months, not one of the new dusters was working. The new duster required oiling and maintenance, a task with which the farmers were unfamiliar. As a result, they went back to their primitive, hard-to-work, but durable duster.

Regardless of the source of the pressures for product modification, the decision rule is the same. The firm must attempt to measure the costs and revenues expected with the standard product and compare them with the expected costs and revenues of the modified product. The firm would choose the product with the most profitable outcome. This rule is easy to state, but difficult to implement because it involves several different forecasts and many different markets. As we saw with Ford's Fiera in Thailand and General Mills' cake mixes in Britain, inaccurate forecasts lead to losses.

Finally, we must note that standardization and adaptation are not the only alternatives in product policy. In those countries where neither approach is feasible, the firm can *create a product* especially for those markets. Of course, the created product should be related to the firm's traditional product expertise because of the difficulties involved in entering both a new market and a new product area simultaneously. A food company might create a new food product for a given foreign market, for example, but it will draw on its existing food processing know-how, as Quaker Oats did with a cereal called Incaparina in Latin America. Similarly, General Motors created their basic transportation vehicle especially for developing country markets, but they drew on their extensive experience in making all kinds of motor vehicles. This alternative of creating special products for foreign markets obviously is profitable only when the markets are of sufficient size.

AUXILIARY PRODUCT FEATURES

Consumers everywhere are concerned not only with the physical product they receive, but also with such product features as package, brand, warranty, and image. Because image is created largely by advertising, we address it in our discussion of promotion in Chapter 8. The other product features we shall look at here.

The Package

Two important roles that packaging plays are to protect the product and to promote the product. Each of these tasks varies internationally. The kind of *protection* the product requires depends on the hazards it will encounter on its journey from the factory to the final consumer. The quality of *transportation services* is one variable. In some African and Latin

American countries, for example, glass containers might be impractical because most of the roads are unpaved and rough. *Climate* is another variable. Packaging that is satisfactory in a temperate climate will often be inadequate for tropical or arctic climates. *Length of time* in distribution is another variable. In developing countries, packaged consumer goods may be in the channel for as much as six months versus only one or two months in the United States. As the length of time involved increases, so does the amount of protection needed. For example, a package of Kellogg's Corn Flakes purchased in Congo tasted like the cardboard box it came in. The product had come from South Africa but was in the channel for many months. The package was unable to protect against both the ravages of time and the oppressive heat and humidity the product had to endure. In countries with similar climates, Quaker Oats countered that problem by using more expensive but more effective vacuum-sealed tins.

The package also has a *promotional* role to play—to encourage consumers to buy the product. The promotional role has several aspects. One is size. Familiar U.S. examples of package size as promotion are the 12-ounce beer bottle, the two- and three-liter soft drink bottle, and jug wine bottles. In foreign markets with different shopping habits or lower incomes, a smaller package size will usually be preferred. In low-income countries, single use-sized packages are not unusual. Procter & Gamble found that many Latin American consumers shop every day and can afford only small amounts of detergent; a top seller is a 100-gram bag—just enough to wash one basket of clothes.

Countries differ in their *preferences for packaging materials.* Thus the relative role of paper, plastic, glass, wood, and metal varies in different markets. Another difference is the consumer's desire for *reusable or dual-use containers.* For example, Sucrets lozenge boxes make for handy storage of sewing kits and other essentials; Quaker Oatmeal containers are made into toy trains, planes, and automobiles; while glass jars are used for everything from drinking glasses to containers for nails and screws. In many other countries such packaging is much more popular, especially in lower-income markets. Even though such packaging is often more expensive, it will find greater sales because the consumer perceives greater total value in the purchase.

Ecological concerns are another variable. In many countries, environmentalists are concerned about returnable containers and aerosol packages. Other countries have different views, so the firm must decide which packaging is appropriate for each kind of market as well as overall environmental and ethical implications of their decisions.

A final international variable in packaging is the *needs of the retailer.* In the United States, large-scale retailing is the norm, with supermarkets, department, and discount stores having large volume outlets. In many other countries, especially in developing economies, retail outlets are smaller in floor space, shelf space, and turnover. Stores with limited space and no self-service have differing package needs from those of a Wal-Mart, Kroger, or Toys'R'Us.

The Label

The package, label, and brand questions are closely related. As the firm enters foreign markets, however, it becomes obvious that each product feature has a different role and different requirements, so we must consider them separately. *Color* relates to both package and label, and color preference is highly influenced by culture. In some countries, black is the color for mourning, whereas in others, white is. Red is a popular color for packaging in some countries, especially communist nations, but not so in others. Green is the color of Islam and popular in Muslim nations. Generally, the colors of a nation's flag are safe colors, but market testing is always prudent for color and esthetic questions in foreign markets. In addition to color, *symbolism* is important. A soft drink marketer got in trouble in Arab markets with one of its products that had a series of six-pointed stars on the label. These stars were felt to be too suggestive of Israel's Star of David.

> An experienced international marketer, Bata Shoe Co., stumbled in its labeling symbolism. More than 50 people were wounded when fundamentalist Muslim protestors in Bangladesh demonstrated against a logo on Bata-made sandals. They said the logo was blasphemous because it resembled the Arabic characters for Allah. The logo was intended—and to western eyes appeared—to be a stylized drawing of three bells. The government banned the sale of the sandals, and the company made a public apology and tried to restore its public image.

Language is such an obvious variable it needs little discussion. In most countries, the copy on the label must be in the official language. In countries such as Canada, Belgium, and Switzerland multilingual labels are required. In any case, if the label carries a promotional message, it is in the marketer's interest to ensure that it communicates the intended message in the appropriate national language(s). *Government* requirements are the major force leading to localized copy in labeling. Governments want the label to inform and protect the consumer, but as noted earlier, each country has somewhat different requirements for achieving that goal. If *literacy* rates are low, pictures and illustrations must be used. Finally, the *interests of the firm* are another force for adapting labels. Apart from advertising, the copy on the package is the major form of communication between the firm and the customer. For packaged consumer goods especially, this medium is too important to be treated lightly. For this reason, labeling can be as idiosyncratic as buyer motivation in different countries. The kind of appeal and illustration that will be effective depends on the national psyche. In the United States, for example, a picture on the Wheaties package of woman golfer Ri Pak would not have the same impact as one of Tiger Woods (except in Korea, where the reverse would be true).

Brands and Trademarks

All of the branding questions a firm faces in its home market are usually faced in each of its foreign markets. For example: Which brand name is best? Should we have a family brand? Or private brands? Because foreign markets are usually smaller, the firm cannot afford the same expense in addressing these questions. Indeed, the most common approach is to try to give domestic brands a global franchise. If this objective can be achieved, marketing advantages and economies are gained. For this reason, the names Ford, Mercedes, and Rolls-Royce are among the most valuable properties these firms own. The same is true for other brand names with a global consumer franchise, such as Coca-Cola, Kodak, Levi Strauss, Chanel, and Sony.

Language problems may encourage firms to find *different* brands for different markets. Sometimes a U.S. brand will have an unfavorable or obscene connotation in another language, or simply be unpronounceable.

Pepsi-Cola had a line of soft drinks in the U.S. market under the Patio name. Marketers felt that Patio had the right recreational image for the U.S. market. When Pepsi marketed these same soft drinks to foreign markets, the name Patio carried a less favorable image in Spanish-speaking countries. The company didn't want to have a different brand name in every country, however, so after some research, the name Mirinda was chosen for Pepsi's noncola drinks in all markets outside North America.

Government versus Company Interests

Companies prefer to use the same brand name in all countries for several reasons. One is the promotional economies of scale they can achieve with a single, international brand. It is more efficient to create one good brand name or trademark for world markets than to devise one for each country. It is cheaper to prepare advertising campaigns and sales literature for one brand name than for several. Also, a greater international consumer franchise is likely to be attached to a single brand name than to multiple brand names.

In these days when promotional media can overlap several countries, a single brand name is necessary to take advantage of this exposure. For example, many companies who use the Olympics as a promotional event could not do so if they did not have an international brand name or trademark. How would Adidas, Coca-Cola, or Seiko promote if they had to have a different brand name in every country? In addition to the media overlap between countries, customer overlap is also needed. Many consumers travel from country to country at least occasionally. Their product loyalty could be lost if they don't recognize the company's brand in another country. Industrial customers often have international operations of their own, and in selling to them in different countries, an international brand name is desirable. Furthermore, when a firm is shipping products to many countries from a single production source, it is more efficient to operate with a single brand name.

The branding issue is particularly important because brands and trademarks are the only form of nonprice competition that is legally protected. In each country the firm can register its brands and trademarks as a form of intellectual property and have, in effect, a worldwide monopoly over their use. As with most monopoly power, profit can be realized from the monopoly of a good brand name or trademark. For this reason, about 40,000 brand name and trademark applications are filed annually by U.S. firms in about 80 countries. While companies are happy about the brand name monopoly power they enjoy, the governments of many developing countries are unhappy about it. Developed countries haven't been concerned because they have their own multinational companies, but Third World governments have complained that international trademark laws give relatively more benefits to the international companies and relatively greater costs to their consumers. UNCTAD, the voice of the Third World, has conducted a study of the subject, and individual countries have taken some action.

The Korean government feels that too much money is leaving the country in payment for foreign patents and trademarks, so they have used various means to reduce the outflow. Foremost and Meadowgold are two U.S. food companies with licensing agreements in Korea. Their application for renewal of their contracts was rejected because the government didn't want to continue payments for the use of their names.

The government of the Philippines was discussing a tax on products with foreign trademarks with the rate going from 10 percent in the first year to 25 percent in the third year. This practice would be a rather effective barrier against the use of foreign brands and trademarks.

The eventual impact of these kinds of actions from Third World countries will be to reduce the use of global brands and force the introduction of more local brands. These actions are being fought by multinational companies, occasionally with the help of their governments, sometimes with success. To attract foreign investment as part of its economic liberalization program, India will now allow the use of foreign brand names. This policy changes the previous law that required foreign firms to use different or hybrid names. Foreign firms may now drop their hybrid or local names with government permission. The move was opposed by the Indian industrial lobby, which fears the combination of foreign advertising budgets and popular brand names.

Brand Piracy

International companies spend a great deal of money building a global franchise for their brands and trademarks. They are frequently successful at this objective, so consumers are often willing to pay some premium for the quality level or status associated with international brands. This success has encouraged many imitators, generally in Third World countries, to sell similar products with the same or similar brand name. For example, one can find red boxes of toothpaste with variations in the spelling of Colgate in many countries. Other targets of pirates are software, music, videos, and brand name clothing.

Levi's success has spawned many imitators selling "Levi's." Most were small firms that produced only 3,000–4,000 units before being closed down. One operation was large scale, however, producing more than 100,000 pairs of jeans. The production was done in Taiwan with the sales network in Europe. Eventually, four Europeans were arrested in Switzerland for trademark infringement.

Warranty

From the *consumer's* point of view, a warranty is part of the product because the consumer expects some specified level of performance from the product, not just a physical object. Nct surprisingly, what consumers expect from a product varies somewhat from country to country because of such factors as the level of development, competitive practice, and the amount of consumerism. From the viewpoint of consumers' expectations, therefore, manufacturer warranties or cars, tires, watches, or machine tools would not always be uniform around the world.

The *manufacturer's* interest in warranties reinforces the trend to have different warranties in different countries. Manufacturers use warranties partly for legal reasons. They promise certain things to the buyer while trying to limit their liability in connection with the product. Legal requirements on warranties vary greatly around the world. Sometimes verbal guarantees can be binding. Manufacturers also use warranties for promotional purposes, promising better performance and/or less trouble than a competing car, computer, or television set. These promotional uses of warranties often differ by country. When a firm has a strong established position in a market, it may offer a weaker warranty than in a market where its product is new or faces strong competition. In some markets the firm may be a warranty leader; in others it may be a warranty follower according to its competitive situation.

In spite of the fragmentation common in international warranty policy, occasionally one will find a uniformity in international warranties. Otis elevators and Boeing aircraft obviously can't have much difference in warranty between countries. Furthermore, various pressures encourage greater uniformity. The forces of growing international competition, economic integration as in the European Union, increased international travel and tourism, and the continued expansion of multinational firms all promote greater international uniformity in warranties.

Service

Postsale service is a critical part of the total product for such consumer goods as automobiles and appliances and for industrial goods such as computers and capital equipment. The service question in international marketing is not whether to offer standardized service, which would be impossible. As any car owner knows, two dealers handling the same make of car don't offer the same service, even in the same city. The question the international marketer asks is, How can we provide good or at least adequate service in our foreign markets?

What constitutes "adequate" service internationally depends on such factors as the level of development, competitive practice, and product use conditions. The service problem is further complicated in international marketing by the fact that, in many markets, the firm itself is not physically present. Rather, it is represented by independent distributors or licensees. Furthermore, for U.S. firms, foreign markets are smaller than the domestic market, so diseconomies of scale may affect international service capability. The geographic and cultural distance between the home market and foreign markets is another complicating factor. All these factors combine to make the task of establishing an international service capability one of the real challenges facing marketers of products requiring after-sale service. At the same time, success awaits those firms who do a good job with service in their foreign markets, such as Caterpillar around the world, and the German and Japanese automakers in the United States.

DEVELOPING PRODUCTS FOR WORLD MARKETS

When firms first begin selling in foreign markets they face two product policy questions: Which of our existing products should we sell abroad? Do we need to adapt our products for foreign customers? We have already discussed how firms answer these questions. As the firm continues in international marketing, it faces a third product policy question: Do we need to internationalize our product development process? Most U.S. firms find that the products coming out of their domestic research and development are not perfectly suited to the needs of world markets. Therefore these products are either not marketable internationally or they must undergo varying degrees of adaptation. One international marketer of industrial goods told the author, 'We make a sophisticated product for the U.S. market, but then take something out to make it less sophisticated for some foreign markets in developing nations. The trouble with this approach is that the less sophisticated product can become more expensive because of redesign work than the one we sell in the United States.' This particular problem does not affect all international marketers, but all face the same basic question: What is the best way to develop products for world markets?

Product Development in Foreign Markets

U.S. firms generally develop products for their home market in domestic research and development (R&D) facilities. To treat foreign markets in the same way would require a product development facility in each of the firm's foreign markets. This strategy is not practiced for several reasons. One reason is that most foreign markets are smaller than the domestic market and cannot support such a facility. Furthermore, not every country has the professional personnel for such an operation. Another reason is that the firm is not physically present in all of its foreign markets. Indeed, generally the firm will be represented by independent local distributors in the majority of its foreign markets. Yet another reason is that most foreign markets are not sufficiently unique to require individualized product development any more than individual consumers generally require customized products.

While it is true that firms do not conduct R&D in each of their foreign markets, it is equally true that firms active in international marketing generally conduct R&D in some of their foreign markets. Furthermore, the percentage of R&D done abroad increases as the firm's international experience grows. Several factors encourage this internationalization of the firm's R&D. One is host government pressure. Governments are uncertain about the balance of costs and benefits of multinational firms, but one activity they always welcome is local R&D. They believe that it increases the technological transfer and contribution of the multinational. They feel strongly enough about local R&D to provide financial incentives. For example, the Canadian government has helped many U.S. firms when they expanded R&D in Canada. NCR began a new facility in Canada and received half the start-up cost as a subsidy from the government. Marketing factors also encourage firms to conduct R&D abroad. To the extent that foreign markets require different products, local R&D helps to find the right products. It can also serve to monitor local technological and competitive developments. These marketing factors apply with greatest force in the larger, more advanced markets of the firm, and it is in these countries that most of the foreign R&D of U.S. companies is done.

Coordinating International Product Development

Multinational firms often have a foreign R&D facility in conjunction with one or more of their foreign factories. Firms that market internationally only via exports or licensing do not find it feasible to conduct R&D abroad. Even the multinationals will have R&D in only a few of their

BOX 5-2   *New Products, New Markets*

Cheerios, Coca-Cola, and Tide are world-renowned brands. They are also distinguished for their longevity. The United States is a large market, one that attracts 20,000–25,000 new products each year. With a failure rate between 80 and 95 percent though, the market place always has room for next year's crop.

U.S. consumers spend more than $3.5 billion on soup annually. New Covent Garden Soup Company, the U.K. affiliate of Glencoe Foods, sees the opportunity for growth by introducing a new soup line into the United States. Covent Garden soups have been doing well in San Francisco, the company's test market. Now, plans include a rollout for the rest of California and select cities in the West. The question is, will Covent Garden be successful?

Even though the United States is a big market, Covent Garden will have to overcome some obstacles if it is to succeed in meeting its goal.

- Competition: Campbell's Soup (38 percent market share, sales of $8 billion) is the largest, but other firms include Progresso (subsidiary of Grand Metropolitan, owner of Pillsbury, Burger King, and IDV), Lipton, Swanson, Knorr, College Inn, Nissin, and store brands.
- Cultural problems: Covent Garden soups require new consumer purchase and use patterns. Their soups are ready to heat and eat (as opposed to those which require adding water or milk); they are freshly made and require refrigeration (with a shelf life of two to three weeks); they are located in the dairy section rather than with other soups; and they are relatively expensive ($3–4 per serving). The soups needed reformulation because they were too salty and had high fat content which were unacceptable to health-conscious Americans. Spicy corn chowder and the black bean with green chile flavors were substituted for the fresh haddock and the Brussels sprouts with chestnut varieties that are sold in England.
- Small marketing budget: Covent Garden cannot afford television or other forms of mass advertising, and relies solely on in-store samples and word of mouth.

Sources: "Got Soup?" *The San Francisco Chronicle* (June 13, 1998), D1;
"Flipping Over Flops," *Chicago Sun-Times* (June 29, 1998), p. 43;
Campbell Soup Company 1997 Annual Report <http://www.campbellsoups.com>;
1996 Annual Review, Grand Metropolitan <http://www.diageo.com/GrandMet96Review>.

markets. Nevertheless, all these firms need to internationalize their product development process if they want to develop appropriate products for world markets.

Before we discuss the internationalization process, a few comments are in order. One relates to *world products*. Coca-Cola is probably as close as one can come to a world product—one that is uniform in all markets.

Firms are rarely fortunate enough to come up with a product that can sell around the world with no adaptation. Nescafé, for example, is another beverage with worldwide sales, but there are dozens of different formulations of Nescafé for different markets. And the other products of the Coca-Cola company do not enjoy as much international uniformity as the company's standard-bearer. Therefore, when we speak of coordinating international product development, the goal is not an internationally uniform product. The automobile industry provides a constructive example.

> General Motors and Ford have developed "world cars." Because of the need for production economies and long production runs, these cars have a high degree of commonality in engines, drive trains, and other expensive components. The sheet metal work and the accessories or options packages, however, allow for customizing to individual national markets. As one General Motors executive said, "You wouldn't even recognize it as the same car." One might call this practice an attempt to maximize uniformity and diversity at the same time.

An internationally uniform product is not usually an attainable goal. The opposite extreme, developing different products for each foreign market, is not an economically attractive goal. Doing different things in different markets leads to diseconomies in both production and marketing. Extreme product diversity destroys much of the synergy that is potentially available in international marketing. Therefore, a reasonable goal for international product development is to try to find the amount of product diversity that will satisfy the firm's markets while retaining economies of scale in production and marketing.

> Hewlett-Packard provides an example of coordinated development and adaptation. Most of the development work on H-P printers is done in the United States, but today they can make a new model available in Asian languages in only 60 days—a process that used to take nine months. H-P accomplishes its task by drawing on its allies and resources in the region. In Japan, the company has a research lab and a manufacturing operation; in Korea, a joint venture with Samsung Electronics; in Singapore, a large printer plant with a strong engineering staff; and in China, alliances with software designers. By coordinating its global resources, Hewlett-Packard can achieve the appropriate degree of standardization and adaptation quickly.

The suggested approach is similar to what companies practice in their domestic markets. Though each customer is unique in some way, firms do not produce unique products for each one. Rather, they group customers into similar groups or segments and develop a limited number of product offerings for this large market.

> For the millions of detergent buyers, Procter & Gamble offers only about five kinds of detergent for that market.
>   The many different sizes and kinds of computer users (banks, retailers, manufacturers, etc.) all have differing needs. However, IBM serves this market with a limited number of computer offerings.

We are suggesting international market segmentation and moderate product diversity as guidelines for international product development. These guidelines are useful both for multinational firms with foreign R&D and for firms who sell abroad only through exports. In either case, they must coordinate their international product development to find products that can be profitably marketed in world markets. *A critical factor in the successful internationalization of product development is some kind of strategic statement and job description to guide the activity.* If the guidelines for product development do not include an international dimension, it is unlikely that product development will make its maximum contribution to the firm's global marketing.

We shall now look at the product development process and consider how the various stages can be internationalized. We will assume that the firm is marketing internationally only by exporting for illustrative purposes. Exhibit 5-3 depicts the various stages in the product development process as we shall discuss them.

Getting Product Ideas

Customers, company technicians and managers, competitors, the salesforce, and distributors are all potential sources of new product ideas. The same should be true in international marketing, but accessing these sources is more difficult to achieve when the firm is not physically present in the foreign market. Means of communication must be established with these idea sources. The *local distributors* must be encouraged to report ideas from their salesforces, local competition, and their own local knowledge. They will probably need incentives for passing along such information, even though they will also benefit indirectly from new products for their markets. Additionally, the *export managers* or other company representatives should periodically visit foreign markets for the same purpose.

EXHIBIT 5-3   *The Product Development Process*

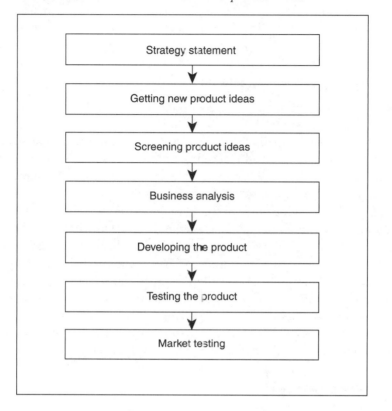

The company traveler should know what is going on in domestic product development to be able to enrich it with ideas and insight from abroad.

Trade fairs are important in many countries and visits to, or participation in, these can be a source of product ideas. Government five-year *development plans* indicate product-market opportunities for many firms. Foreign *trade and technical publications* are another kind of idea source from foreign markets. Obviously, getting product ideas from foreign markets is more difficult than from domestic operations. It can be done, however, and without exorbitant costs. We have suggested several idea sources. The most expensive is international travel by a representative of the firm; however, their multipurpose natures make the cost of these international marketing trips only partly assignable to new product development.

For example, Unilever has a three-person team looking for new products to aid company growth. They scour the world for food ideas that can be transplanted from one market to another. They are aided by Unilever's extensive international presence.

Screening Product Ideas

The firm cannot afford to develop every new product idea, so it must choose the ideas with the highest probability of success. Product ideas are screened to evaluate their compatibility with company goals, company image, and its production and marketing capabilities which may vary from market to market. The screening process is complicated for the international marketer because all criteria generally vary from country to country or between the domestic and foreign markets. If the firm has production abroad, its evaluation of the production compatibility of the new product idea will be quite different from that of a firm with only domestic production. These differences have two implications for the screening of new product ideas. One is that the evaluators must consider the firm's goals and capabilities in *all* markets. Second, successful screening requires input from foreign distributors and subsidiaries to take advantage of their local market knowledge. This gathering of information may be done in part during trips by international marketing staff.

Business Analysis

The business analysis of new product ideas could be considered part of the screening process, but it is often discussed separately. If the product idea scores well on the screening criteria just noted, its probable business success must be analyzed. Its future sales, costs, and profits must be estimated. For the firm selling internationally, *sales estimates* must be prepared for a number of markets. International marketing personnel at the home office will participate in these estimates, but the figures will be more realistic if foreign distributors and subsidiaries contribute their expertise. *Cost figures* include production and marketing costs. Production costs are relatively easy to estimate if all production is domestic. If the firm has foreign production facilities, estimating costs becomes more difficult but also more interesting because a multinational producer has more alternatives than a purely national producer. Marketing costs will vary from country to country because of differing market share, product line, marketing program, and kind of involvement (distributor, licensee, or subsidiary).

All these elements make business analysis of new product ideas more difficult for international marketers. However, it also makes it more rewarding because of the increased opportunities and alternatives available in world markets.

Developing the Product

When new product idea is introduced that promises attractive future profits, actual development of the physical product can begin. For the firm with production only in its home market, the issue is fairly straightforward. However, the firm with multinational production is faced with more varied possibilities. It can choose from among various country candidates according to differences in capacity availability, cost structures, technical expertise and personnel, and perhaps government incentive programs.

> Unisys has engineering centers in five countries. Once many of their new product ideas reach this stage, they let the engineering centers bid for the development of the new product. Different bids are submitted according to the various centers' capacity situation, interest, and particular expertise. This procedure appears to assure that development will be assigned where it can be done most effectively and efficiently.

Another advantage of having multiple product development centers is that large-scale or crash projects can be split up for faster development. For example, IBM and Honeywell both practiced an extensive international division of labor in bringing a new generation of computers to the market. Today, many firms form strategic alliances to take advantage of that international division of labor.

> Otis Elevator developed a special elevator by using six research centers in five countries. A U.S. team handled systems integration, the Japanese team designed the special motor drives, German engineers handled the electronics, and the Spanish group did the small-geared components. Otis says the international effort saved $10 million in design costs and cut development time from four years to two.

Testing the Product

As the product is being developed, it must be tested to assure that it does what it is supposed to do. Industrial goods must meet certain standards of performance and reliability. Consumer goods also must meet performance standards, as well as address consumers' concerns about subjective dimensions such as taste, style, and image. For industrial goods, climate, operating conditions, and maintenance practices vary internationally. For consumer goods, these types of differences are issues along with the addition of variability in consumer tastes and product expectations. All these differences suggest that the international marketer will frequently find it necessary to test products in selected foreign markets as well as at home. These markets should be representative of the differing uses and operating conditions facing the firm's product. Problems can arise from failure to test a product in a major foreign market.

A Japanese industrial marketer was selling equipment to U.S. factories and received many complaints. One complaint was based on Americans' taller and heavier stature. This difference from home market specifications necessitated size and structural changes in the equipment. Another complaint arose from the U.S. practice of longer hours and more intensive use of the machinery, which caused frequent breakdowns not found in Japan. The equipment had to be reengineered and strengthened.

Market Testing the Product

The rationale of market testing is well known. The firm wants to be assured that the product will pass the ultimate test—customers buy it—before making great commitments in production facilities and marketing launch costs. The same logic applies in international marketing because production commitments and marketing costs are also a reality for foreign markets. The problem is obvious because the great number of foreign markets for the firm, all of which are smaller than the domestic market, make market testing itself an expensive undertaking. The answer is not to avoid test marketing, but to apply the principle of selecting a small number of countries that are representative of the firm's international markets, just as test market cities in the United States are used to represent the whole national market. This representative sample could be derived by choosing, say, a country in Europe, one in Latin America, and one in Asia. Belgium is often used as a test market for Europe, for example.

Instead of using whole countries, even small ones, as test markets, cities or regions of countries could be used. Unilever used a selected region of France to represent all western Europe when successfully market testing a new toilet soap. The challenge here is to *find* those representative countries or regions. They will not be the same for all products or firms. The international marketer must do a comparative analysis of the firm's markets to determine which markets are representative of different categories of customers. Some approaches to such comparative analysis were discussed in Chapter 4.

SUMMARY

The existence of world markets offers great profit potential for firms that can market their products there. Generally, however, firms cannot merely extend their domestic products to foreign markets. Various kinds of adaptation may be necessary in the physical product itself or in its packaging, branding, and warranty. We have discussed the considerations involved in product adaptation, noting how firms try to minimize the amount and costs of such modification while finding products that are still appropriate for different world markets. We then looked at product development in the firm and discussed how internationalizing this activity could lead to more profitable marketing abroad. The steps in the product development process were analyzed to see how they could be coordinated internationally to better develop products suitable for both domestic and foreign markets.

QUESTIONS

1. Why do firms prefer to sell their standard domestic products in foreign markets?
2. What is the significance of the international product life cycle for international marketers?
3. Discuss some of the factors that force firms to adapt their products for world markets.
4. Why do firms frequently find it necessary to modify their packaging for foreign markets?
5. Discuss the problem of brand piracy.
6. Why do multinational firms develop products primarily in their domestic R&D facilities?
7. Which factors encourage firms to conduct some R&D in foreign markets?
8. Why is it usually unnecessary for firms to develop new products for each world market?
9. How can firms get new product ideas from world markets to guide their R&D activity?

FURTHER READING

1. Cateora, Philip R. and John L. Graham, *International Marketing*, 10th ed. (Boston, MA: Irwin/McGraw-Hill, 1999), Chapters 12 and 13.
2. Crawford, C. Merle, *New Products Management*, 3rd ed. (Homewood, IL: Irwin, 1991).
3. "P&G's Pepper Spells Out Strategic Importance of China," *Advertising Age International* (May 14, 1998) <http://adage.com/international/ daily>.
4. Colaveski, John M., "Great Plains Joins Software Vendors Going 'Over There'," *Accounting Today*, vol. 11, no. 19 (October 20, 1997), p. 26.
5. Jain, Subhash C., *International Marketing Management*, 5th ed. (Cincinnati: South-Western College Publishing, 1996), Chapter 12.
6. Terpstra, Vern, and Ravi Sarathy, *International Marketing*, 7th ed. (Fort Worth, TX: Dryden Press, 1997), Chapters 8 and 9.

NOTE: Basic marketing texts usually devote one or more chapters to product policy.

C H A P T E R   6

International Distribution Decisions

D omestic marketing manuals approach the question of distribution from the viewpoint of the producer who wants to reach customers in their home market, that is, the producer and the customers are in the same country. In international marketing, the producer and the customers may not be in the same country, which creates quite a different set of distribution challenges for the firm: How do we get our products *into* foreign markets? How do we choose and manage distribution channels *within* foreign markets? How do we manage physical distribution for world markets? This discussion of international distribution will focus on these three issues.

GETTING PRODUCTS INTO FOREIGN MARKETS

In addition to geographic separation, foreign markets are separated from the domestic market in other significant ways: legally, financially, and culturally. Overcoming these barriers makes the problem of getting products into foreign markets one of the biggest challenges facing the international marketer. We must not exaggerate the difficulty of the task, however; because of the many different ways to enter foreign markets, a firm wishing

119

BOX 6-1   *Global Retailing: IKEA on the Move*

IKEA announced it is opening nine showrooms in Russia, a second store in Beijing, and six new stores throughout eastern Europe. It is also about to open its first retail furniture showroom in Scotland.

IKEA, founded in 1943 by 17-year-old Ingvar Kamprand, began selling high-quality, inexpensive furniture by mail order in 1950. Three years later, Mr. Kamprand opened the first showroom in Sweden. Billed as the only global furniture chain, one can find IKEA stores throughout most of Europe, eastern Europe (in Hungary and Poland since 1990), the Middle East (in Saudi Arabia since 1983), Asia (in Australia since 1975), and North America (in Canada since 1976). The first store in the United States was opened nearly ten years later (1985), and in 1998 IKEA opened its first store in China.

IKEA relies heavily on imports and exports for moving supplies and goods around the world. Sales in 1997 were in excess of US $6 billion, 84 percent coming from Europe and the Middle East, 14 percent from North America, and 1 percent from Asia. On the other hand, materials used in constructing the furniture and other items come from more than 2,400 suppliers located in more than 65 countries. The bulk of materials (32 percent) originate from continental Europe; 28 percent comes from the Nordic countries, 20 percent from Asia, 17 percent from central Europe, and 3 percent from North America.

The opening of a store typically means about 250 new jobs to the area, but despite the expected boost to the local economy, IKEA is not always met with open arms. For example, the application to locate the store near Glasgow was denied by the Secretary of State for Scotland and some attribute the denial to IKEA's very success—their stores tend to generate a lot of traffic and hence tie up roadways. However, they did finally get approval to locate further east in less congested Straiton, Midlothian, and the introduction of the low-priced, high-quality furniture retail outlet is going ahead as scheduled.

Sources: Justin Ryan and Colin Mcallister, "Lie Back and Think of Sweden," *The Herald* (Glasgow), (September 12, 1998), p. 20; Paul de Bendern, "Secretive Ikea Plans Global Expansion," *Calgary Herald* (August 10, 1998), p. C1; <http://www.ikea.com/content/main.>.

to market abroad can probably find a suitable method, regardless of the company's size and circumstances. We cannot cover here all the possible ways of getting products into foreign markets, but we shall give an overview of the major alternatives. The firm can choose the entry method that best suits its own situation and goals.

Before discussing the various entry methods, we want to stress the importance of careful planning in making this decision. The choice of entry method for foreign markets is one of the most important international decisions the firm makes. It is something like the marriage decision for an individual. Both decisions involve certain commitments that are not easily reversed. Furthermore, in both cases, the one big decision effectively influences or determines the outcome of a lot of other decisions at the same time. The choice of entry method to a great extent constrains the firm's ability to do marketing research, its choice of product strategies, and its pricing and other marketing functions in foreign markets. Some entry methods allow the firm no voice in its marketing program in the foreign market, as with indirect exporting or licensing. Other entry methods give the firm varying degrees of control over its international marketing, such as exporting or foreign marketing subsidiaries. Thus, the choice of entry method into foreign markets largely determines the international marketing task facing the firm.

MARKETING INTERNATIONALLY FROM DOMESTIC PRODUCTION

The majority of international marketing today is carried out by firms that sell to foreign markets from their domestic factories. Many firms lack the resources to acquire factories abroad, or they fear the problems and risks associated with production in foreign countries. These firms then find some way to reach foreign markets with the products of their domestic factories. A firm has several options in how it can market its products internationally as shown in Exhibit 6-1.

Domestic Sales for Foreign Markets

It is not only possible to serve foreign markets from domestic production, but also possible to serve foreign markets from the domestic sales organization. That is, a U.S. firm can consummate the sale within the United States. This kind of international marketing is obviously the easiest and involves the least commitment from the firm. We will note some of the approaches to this kind of international marketing.

Foreign Buyers in the Domestic Market

Many foreign business organizations have procurement offices in the United States. Large foreign *retail or wholesale organizations* are examples. Various items in their product lines are of foreign origin, and they find it efficient to maintain buying offices in major supplier countries,

EXHIBIT 6-1 *Serving Foreign Markets from Domestic Production*

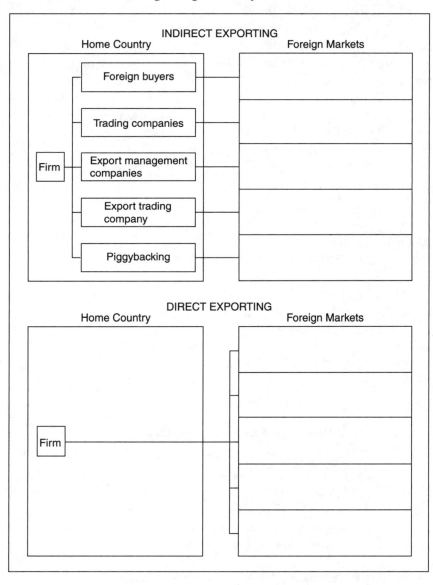

especially because many firms from whom they buy are small and unsophisticated international marketers. Sears and Macy's are U.S. firms with such foreign buying offices. Foreign firms in *manufacturing and extractive industries* will also frequently have a procurement office in the United States. They seek supplies and equipment rather than items for resale, but their reasons for such offices are basically the same as for the retailers and wholesalers.

International Trading Companies

International traders, such as the Japanese Mitsubishi or Mitsui, also have U.S. buying offices. These companies are major suppliers of foreign goods to the markets they serve. The Japanese trading companies account for half of Japan's imports, and the United Africa Company is a leading importer into many African nations. Trading companies may handle an extremely wide range of both consumer and industrial goods, from cosmetics to chemicals, cars to computers. They specialize in the buying and selling of goods rather than the production of goods. The large trading companies carry on their business in many different countries.

> Itochu is one of the largest Japanese trading companies (founded by Chubei Ito and formerly known as C. Itoh & Company). In 1997, the company announced the construction of a new headquarters building in Osaka. The Cosmo Square complex will also house the Asia-Pacific Trade Center and the World Trade Center. This facility will aid foreign exporters' entry into Japan by bringing together in one place major Japanese distributors, exporters from around the world, and export-related resources, all connected to the rest of the world using the most advanced global communications network.

U.S. Multinationals

Sometimes multinationals provide a similar avenue to foreign markets. When they produce goods or build factories abroad, they often continue to buy components or capital equipment from their domestic suppliers. Because many of these suppliers do not have foreign factories, the procurement will be done in the United States. In all these cases, the firm is making domestic sales, but its products are ending up in foreign markets. Although this method provides an easy way to market internationally, it may not be optimal. The seller is dependent on the products and markets of interest to the *buying* organization. This strategy could leave many products and markets uncovered in terms of the international opportunities facing the firm.

As a successful example of this approach, Systems Center Inc., of Virginia began its international sales by selling its software to U.S. multinationals for their overseas operations. This move led to an international network of 39 agents overseas, which accounted for more than half of its total sales.

Export Management Companies

An export management company (EMC) is a firm that manages exports for other firms. It produces no products of its own, but rather serves as an international marketing intermediary. It acts as the export department of the firm and may even use its letterhead. Using an EMC offers several potential advantages to the producing firm. The EMC can give instant knowledge of foreign markets and international marketing know-how. This asset can be particularly important for the firm with no previous international experience. By handling several complementary lines, the EMC gains economies of scale in shipping and foreign market representation. Use of an EMC saves the firm the time and expense of establishing its own export department. The EMC usually sells on a commission basis, making it a variable cost operation. The EMC route also offers more producer control than do foreign resident buyers. In theory, the EMC appears to be an ideal way for the small or medium-sized firm to begin marketing internationally. In practice, however, all of the promised performance and advantages may not be realized. Nevertheless, the EMC approach should be considered by smaller firms contemplating international marketing. More than 1,000 EMCs operate in the United States. Initial information can be obtained from field offices of the U.S. Department of Commerce.

> Heat Sealing Equipment & Manufacturing Company of Cleveland, Ohio, manufactures specialized packaging equipment and supplies. One of their subsidiaries, AMPAK sells machinery worldwide through a network of business-to-business distributors. When they first entered a new market, however, and lacked the experience to sell their products directly to industrial buyers, they used EMCs for global distribution.

Export Trading Companies

American concern about the continuing trade deficit led to the passage of the Export Trading Company Act in 1982. It permitted firms to join together for export while enjoying antitrust protection. Because EMCs have a rather small role in U.S. exports, the government wanted a more powerful way to help U.S. exporters. It was an attempt to emulate the Japanese trading companies, which play such a big role in Japanese exports. It allowed giant banks or corporations with wide international experience to form an export trading company (ETC). Smaller firms that join the ETC benefit from the great resources and international network of the major bank or corporate member. Bank of America, Citicorp, and General Motors are among the large firms that have formed ETCs. Results of these ventures are not impressive. The General Electric and Sears trading companies have discontinued operations and the other U.S. ETCs have failed to match the success of the Japanese trading companies.

Piggyback Exporting

Another kind of domestic sale for foreign markets is piggyback exporting. A firm with excess capacity in its exporting or international marketing operations may seek out complementary products to sell abroad to improve the efficiency and profitability of those operations. The logic here is similar to that behind an EMC or an ETC: enhanced profitability through economies of scale. Both carrier and rider seek the kinds of advantages found in the other forms of cooperative exporting. Borg-Warner, Colgate, General Electric, and Schick are companies that have carried other firms' products abroad. Cyanamid, DuPont, in-Sink-Erator, and McGraw Edison are examples of companies whose products have been carried abroad in this way. DuPont generally does its own international marketing of chemicals, of course, except for one consumer product, Reveal Wrap, which they piggyback with Colgate.

> Avon in Latin America provides a good illustration of the logic and benefits of piggybacking for both carrier and rider. Avon operates in fifteen countries in Latin America and the Caribbean, and has more than 500,000 sales representatives there. This potent marketing force combined with an effective distribution system has given Avon sales of over $1.8 billion for its International Americas division. With this well-established marketing network, Avon has the capacity to sell other complementary products that can expand its sales and profits with little incremental cost. By the same token, other manufacturers can benefit from piggybacking on Avon's strong marketing presence at a low marginal cost to themselves. It would cost them dearly to establish such a marketing presence for their own product. As a result, Avon formed piggyback alliances in Latin America with such other U.S. companies as CBS Records, S. C. Johnson, and Corning.

Foreign Sales for Foreign Markets

We have been discussing what might be called *indirect exporting,* the firm's products enter foreign markets with little or no international marketing effort or investment by the firm. In spite of the advantages of these indirect ways of entering foreign markets, many firms prefer to enter foreign markets directly and do their own export marketing. We call this method *direct exporting.* It means that the firm itself undertakes the complete export marketing task, which is extensive. Direct exporting includes choosing appropriate foreign markets; selecting agents or distributors to represent the firm in those markets; motivating and controlling those distributors; choosing the product line for the target markets; setting prices and determining promotional strategies for those markets; handling international shipping, insurance, and finance; and preparing export documentation.

Obviously direct exporting is more demanding and expensive than indirect exporting. Why, then, do so many firms choose this way of entering foreign markets? Presumably they feel the extra benefits are greater than the increased costs. Direct exporting increases costs in several categories: establishing an *export department* requires extra staff and space; more capital is required to carry *export inventories and accounts receivable* than with indirect exporting; foreign *travel* will be necessary; extra *risk* accompanies long-distance, cross-cultural dealings that include international shipping, credit, and foreign exchange transactions. The extra benefits are few in number but may be compelling. The major argument would be increased control, which can lead to greater sales and profits from direct exporting. The firm is handling only its own products and gives them its full effort and attention, meaning greater sales. The firm can choose the products and markets most appropriate to its international goals. Finally, the firm is learning about world markets and international marketing—knowledge that is invaluable for continued international business growth.

3M Company illustrates how a company can begin its international marketing with modest direct exporting and become a large multinational company. 3M began by exporting sandpaper and adhesive tape. Its strategy in entering a country is to begin with one basic product. Two examples are reflective sheeting for traffic signs in Russia and scouring pads in Hungary. Then it adds new products, one at a time, as it gains experience and knowledge of the market. This developmental strategy has worked well for 3M. By 1997, the company was exporting 50,000 different products to nearly 200 countries. Even more important, total international sales were $7.8 billion, or more than half of total sales ($15.1 billion). As 3M learned about foreign markets and international marketing through its export experience, it became a full-fledged multinational company processing or producing a large percent of its products within the foreign markets.

MARKETING INTERNATIONALLY
FROM FOREIGN PRODUCTION

Manufacturers who market internationally generally prefer to serve foreign markets from their domestic plants. Their reasons are not simply xenophobic but economic and political. Foreign factories require capital to build. Furthermore, this capital is at risk in a foreign environment. Sometimes U.S. firms find their foreign facilities threatened because of an unpopular action of the U.S. government—Yankee, go home! As someone said, "If you don't have foreign factories, they can't be bombed or expropriated." Foreign production also involves costs in learning to operate in an unfamiliar labor and legal environment. Some foreign markets may be too small for an economically sized plant. Not only U.S. firms reason this way. For example, before foreign automakers locate factories in the United States, they export most of the cars sold in the United States from their facilities in their home countries.

While many forces encourage international marketers to keep their production at home, many countervailing pressures encourage them to produce abroad. High transportation costs might make a domestically produced product too expensive for a foreign market. Similarly, import duties can raise the product's price, making it noncompetitive. In both cases, local production may be the only way the firm can lower costs enough to compete in the market. Many governments have "Buy National" policies, requiring local production to serve that market. These factors might be called negative inducements to produce locally, but a number of factors act as positive incentives to establishing foreign factories. Production costs may be lower abroad. The firm can learn more of local market needs and give better service by being close to the market. Host governments may provide financial incentives and other preferential treatment to firms that produce in their country. The net result of all these considerations is that thousands of firms have some kind of foreign production to serve foreign markets. We shall consider the major approaches as shown in Exhibit 6-2.

Licensing

Licensing is a form of foreign production by proxy. In a licensing agreement, the international marketing firm gives something of value to the licensee, such as blueprints, patents, brand names and/or know-how, and in return, the licensee agrees to produce and market the product(s) in its country. The licensor, the international firm, thus avoids the capital investment, legal, and labor

EXHIBIT 6-2   *Alternate Ways of Serving Foreign Markets from Foreign Production*

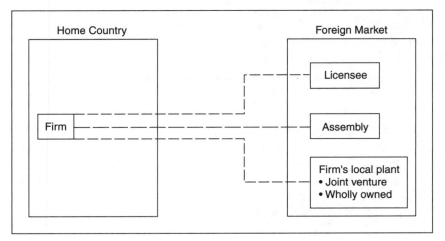

problems normally associated with foreign production. Because the licensee also does the marketing in its country, the licensor has a minimal international involvement. Along with this minimal involvement goes a modest return to the licensor. Five percent royalty on licensee sales of the product(s) covered by the agreement is a typical arrangement. Licensees generally like this approach because it allows access to established products that are either protected by patents or brand names, or would be costly to develop in-house. Licensees usually gain new technology as well.

Because of its advantages to both parties, licensing is a common form of international marketing. However, although it is the quickest, cheapest, and easiest route to foreign production and marketing, most licensors have reservations about it. One concern is the relatively low rate of return. The licensor feels it is giving up the firm's most valuable possession, its know-how, and getting only a small percent of sales in return. The second, more serious concern is the fear of establishing a competitor. Licensing agreements usually run for less than ten years, often only five years. Unless the product is protected by brand names or long-run patents, it is possible that the licensee, having become expert in an item's production, will continue to produce and market it after the agreement expires without paying royalties to the licensor. This behavior is legal, but it is also the nightmare of every licensor. Many U.S. executives complain about their experience with licensing, especially in the case of Japan. A common refrain is, "We gave our best R&D and know-how to Japan for about 5 percent of sales. In less than a decade they came back and beat us in our own market."

Company-Owned Foreign Production

When the firm wants factories in foreign markets and it does not choose to license a local producer there, its primary alternative is some kind of company-owned production facility. Operations in such a facility may range from assembly to complete manufacture. Ownership may range from a joint venture with a local partner in the country to complete ownership by the international firm. We shall consider the international marketing implications of various kinds of operations and ownership.

Assembly versus Complete Manufacturing

Assembly operations are less expensive and complicated than complete manufacturing. They may, however, be sufficient to save transportation costs and duties and satisfy local governments. Firms generally prefer assembly to complete manufacturing in foreign markets, not only because it is cheaper, but also because it allows most of the production, value added, and technology to remain in the home country where it can be better controlled. On the other hand, the advantage of complete manufacturing abroad is that it permits better adaptation of the firm's products and product line to the local market, an important marketing consideration.

> For many years, the Japanese made light trucks that underwent partial assembly—attaching the truck bed to the body—in the United States. This limited degree of assembly was sufficient to earn them a 3 percent duty rather than the 25 percent duty on assembled trucks. Later, U.S. customs officials decided that this limited assembly operation did not warrant the 3 percent duty on "unassembled" vehicles and began charging the full 25 percent duty. This full duty forced the Japanese producers to consider more extensive assembly or manufacturing operations in the United States such as we now see in the U.S. plants of Honda, Mazda, Nissan, and Toyota.

Joint Ventures versus Whole Ownership

Many firms prefer 100 percent ownership of their foreign facilities. In 1978, IBM left India rather than compromise on this point. Complete ownership means greater control and flexibility, easier and better coordination of multicountry operations, and no conflicts with national partners who have different methods and objectives. One drawback to full ownership is that it is more expensive. A firm can have twice as many factories with 50 percent ownership as with 100 percent ownership. Another drawback is that many countries will not allow the firm to enter unless it shares ownership with local investors. Thus some markets may be closed if the firm insists on full ownership. General Motors and IBM have policies strongly favoring full ownership of their foreign ventures. However, IBM entered a 50–50 joint venture with Tata Industries and reestablished on-shore operations in India in 1993. General Motors also modified its ownership policy to be able to enter certain markets, such as Japan and Korea.

Compared to wholly owned operations, joint ventures abroad have special attractions and disadvantages. In addition to lowering the capital burden on the multinational firm, joint ventures usually mean a quicker entry into the foreign market. The potential local partner probably already has a labor force, production facilities, and a marketing network. They may provide a cultural bridge, contributing instant knowledge of local business and marketing practices. Also, the local partner may serve as a political buffer helping the multinational avoid mistakes and making its presence less visible and onerous. The major disadvantage in joint ventures is that the national partner is likely to have different objectives from the multinational firm. The latter wants to optimize on a global basis, while the national partner is interested only in its own market. Furthermore, the national partner's existing product lines and marketing methods may not be a perfect fit with those of the multinational, which may constrain the product choices of the international marketer and pose the problem of teaching the national partner new methods. Given all these considerations, the best counsel is that in joint ventures, as in marriage, great care must be taken to find a compatible partner.

Review of Entry Methods

The initial distribution question in international marketing is how to get the firm's products *into* the foreign market. We have provided an overview of the major methods of entering foreign markets. Each entry method has its strengths and limitations. No absolute rules or easy formulas assure the correct choice. It depends on the situation, the needs of the firm, and the characteristics of the particular entry method. In other words, a case-by-case analysis is necessary. Our discussion has noted many of the variables to be considered in such an analysis.

DISTRIBUTION CHANNELS WITHIN FOREIGN MARKETS

Once a firm has decided on a method to get its products into foreign markets, it faces the second distribution question, How do we distribute our products within those markets? This issue is similar to the one faced domestically. In every country, the producer must decide whether to reach its customers directly or to use one or more intermediaries. Wholesalers and retailers are the principal kinds of intermediaries in world markets just as they are in the domestic market. Thus, the international marketer is on relatively familiar ground when addressing the management of distribution *within* a foreign market. For this reason, our discussion will focus on the *distinctive* aspects of distribution management in world markets.

Impact of Entry Method

We noted earlier that the choice of entry method into foreign markets is one of the most important international business decisions a firm makes. One reason for its importance is that when the firm has chosen its method of entry into a market, in most cases it has also automatically decided on its distribution channels there. In those cases where the firm is not physically present in the foreign market, it is not in charge of its distribution channels there. Someone else is. Only in countries where the firm has its own marketing subsidiary can it choose and manage local distribution channels. If it enters the market some other way, it will have little or no voice in channel selection. We shall review the entry methods to see how they affect the firm's ability to manage distribution within the foreign market.

Domestic Sales for Foreign Markets

When the U.S. firm sells products within the United States and those products end up in foreign markets, the firm is obviously far removed from the distribution channels in those markets. It must rely on the intermediaries located in the United States, not only for its distribution, but also for its complete marketing program abroad. When the firm uses an *export management company* or a *piggyback exporting* arrangement, it can have some voice in its foreign marketing, but it can do little about the distribution channels used abroad. The logic of these arrangements depends on the economies of scale realized from distributing complementary products. Therefore, the firm choosing one of these entry methods must accept the distribution channels being used when it joins. In these cases of indirect exporting, the voice of an individual producer will depend on its share of the sales of the cooperating group.

Direct Exporting

This method affords the firm more influence on distribution channels abroad because the firm is handling only its own products and making its own foreign market contacts. Even the direct exporter, however, has limited management power over distribution in the foreign market. Most direct exporters choose an independent distributor as their representative in the foreign country. These distributors carry the compatible lines of a number of producers. The distributor operates the distribution channels appropriate to its mix of products. An exporter must accept the channels offered by the distributor. If it doesn't like what the distributor offers, the exporter's alternative is to seek out another distributor, which may be difficult. A distributor will not create a channel for the exporter unless a large and profitable volume of business is involved.

Licensing

Foreign production of the firm's product(s), but with little marketing control by the licensor, is the reality of a licensing arrangement. The licensee manufactures the products of the licensor and markets them along with the other products it makes. The licensor accepts the channels offered by the licensee. As with the distributor, the licensee is unlikely to create channels for the licensor without the potential for a large volume of business.

Joint Ventures

Joint ventures abroad give the firm a presence in the foreign market with an ownership interest and thus a voice in local management, including the choice of distribution channels. The greater the equity interest, generally, the greater is the control over distribution channel selection and management. As the name implies, however, a sharing of ownership and management with a national firm is part of the arrangement. This sharing of management constrains somewhat the freedom of the international firm to manage distribution in the joint venture market.

Wholly Owned Foreign Operations

Wholly owned foreign production or marketing operations are the only kind of entry method that gives the firm complete freedom and responsibility in the management of distribution abroad. With 100 percent ownership, the firm, for the first time, replicates in a foreign market its situation in its home market—full responsibility for marketing. Therefore it faces the same distribution questions as at home: What intermediaries should be used? What degree of selectivity is desired? How can we motivate and control the channel? The *approach* to answering these questions is also the same abroad as at home. What we must note here, however, is that the *answers* to these questions may differ in foreign markets because of the different conditions facing the firm. One of these conditions is the size of the foreign market and the firm's business there. Another is the nature of wholesale and retail institutions in world markets. We shall now consider these constraints on international distribution management from the viewpoint of the firm doing its own marketing in foreign markets.

Size of the Firm's Business in the Foreign Market

Two hundred years ago, Adam Smith noted an important theory in economics and marketing: specialization is limited by the size of the market. That idea has two implications for international distribution management. One implication is that in small foreign markets the firm cannot afford direct or extensive distribution. In markets such as Bolivia and Liberia, for example, international firms will rarely have a production or marketing subsidiary. Instead, they will cover those markets through indirect or direct exporting. Goodyear, for example, has many foreign marketing subsidiaries; however, they have also covered a number of small markets through indirect exporting.

A second implication of Smith's theory is that even in large markets, a firm with a small volume of business cannot afford direct or extensive distribution. Two examples will best illustrate this situation—one is a U.S. firm, and the other is a Dutch firm.

General Foods does a business of several billion dollars a year in the United States. They have direct and extensive distribution in this market. General Foods also operates in Japan, another large market, but one in which their volume of business was small. Their market share in Japan was only a fraction of that of the Nestlé company, a competitor in both coffee and processed foods. Both companies, however, practiced a direct form of distribution from factory to retailer. Its small volume made that kind of distribution unprofitable for General Foods.

In order to increase the volume of business to the level necessary to support its desired form of distribution, General Foods finally entered a joint venture with a Japanese food company that was twenty times as large as its own Japanese subsidiary. By piggybacking on the extensive distribution network of its Japanese partner, General Foods was able to reduce unit costs and increase both market share and profitability.

Océ-Nederland B.V. (pronounced *O.K.-Naderlant*) is a Dutch manufacturer of varied products for industrial and commercial markets. Océ established a subsidiary in the United States to sell its products in the U.S. market. The company developed a dry paper copier that it thought would have a big market in the United States. It considered distributing this new product through its U.S. subsidiary but soon realized that its small volume would not enable it to get comprehensive or direct distribution in this large market. The solution chosen was to piggyback with Pitney Bowes, which had excellent coverage of the market because of the widespread sales of its postage meter.

Firms with marketing subsidiaries in foreign markets, such as General Foods and Océ, have complete responsibility for managing distribution in those markets. As our examples show, however, they do not have complete freedom. Their choice of distribution channels is constrained by the volume of their business in the market. Because a firm's sales and market share vary from country to country, the international marketer can expect some similar variation in distribution channels.

WHOLESALING AND RETAILING IN WORLD MARKETS

Culture is the distinctive way of life of a people. Culture affects not only marriage customs, family, and social organization, but also the economy of the country, comprising the agricultural, industrial, and commercial sectors. Every country has marriage customs and family structures, but they differ from country to country. In similar fashion, every country has wholesaling and retailing institutions that also differ internationally. Wholesaling and retailing are not identical in any two countries of the world; however, patterns and similarities can be found. Describing the nature of wholesaling and retailing in all world markets is not possible here. Nevertheless, the consumer marketer must analyze wholesaling and retailing structures in those markets in which the firm has responsibility for distribution management. Here we shall provide an introductory view of the international variations in distribution infrastructure, beginning with wholesaling.

Wholesaling

Wholesaling patterns in world markets are diverse, reflecting the cultures and economies in which they are found. As a rough generalization, one can say that wholesaling varies according to a nation's level of economic development. The developing countries tend to have smaller, more fragmented wholesaling. One finds, for example, that in Iraq and Turkey the average wholesaler has fewer than two employees. Many African nations that rank low on the development scale may still offer larger-scale, efficient wholesaling. In Kenya, for example, the average wholesaler employs more than 12 people, and Uganda averages 18 people per establishment. In many former English colonies the United Africa Company, a Unilever affiliate, offers broad, sophisticated wholesaling coverage. Many former French colonies in Africa are served by large French wholesalers. This situation leads to many developing countries having a mix of strong, large-scale wholesalers, frequently of European origin, alongside hundreds of small local wholesalers.

Many developed countries don't have well-developed wholesaling institutions. Many countries around the world have large numbers of small wholesalers. Because wholesaling benefits from economies of scale, dealing with small wholesalers means less service and a greater burden for the producer. Where the marketer has to deal with small wholesalers, the following problems will generally arise:

1. Instead of providing *credit* to the channel, the wholesaler may be a demander of credit, placing a financial burden on the manufacturer.
2. Small wholesalers carry a narrow *assortment* of goods, which may force the manufacturer to omit some products from the line or seek out other wholesalers to carry them.
3. Small wholesalers offer limited geographic *coverage;* the marketer can either forget about covering the whole national market or try to find other wholesalers for the neglected regions.
4. The resources of small wholesalers limit *service* in other ways too; they carry less inventory; they are generally less effective with selling and promotional efforts; they provide less market feedback to the producer.

In markets with fragmented wholesaling structures, the firm must resign itself to incomplete market coverage or try to overcome the weakness by using a pull strategy, company distribution, or other means. (A pull strategy involves heavy consumer advertising to pull products through the channel.) When facing fragmented wholesaling in Italy, Procter & Gamble took a twofold approach: they emphasized their traditional pull strategy and inserted an extra level in the channel, using a master wholesaler who reached smaller wholesalers who contacted the retailers. U.S. firms usually find Japanese channels of distribution the most complex and contorted in the world. For many, the best answer is to find a Japanese partner as a guide, as General Foods did in our earlier example.

Retailing

As with wholesaling, retailing shows great international diversity. The most significant feature abroad is large numbers of small retailers. However, the retail structure also tends to vary with the nation's level of economic development. More highly-developed countries have more specialty stores, supermarkets, and department stores. They have fewer peddlers, and open air markets play a smaller role. While these observations apply generally around the world, exceptions are numerous. Some developed countries have as much small-scale retailing as developing countries. For all of its economic achievements, Japan, for example, has a fragmented retail structure. Italy is still a nation of small shopkeepers. In Belgium, one pharmacy serves 2,000 people while the Netherlands has only one pharmacy for every 10,000 inhabitants—a remarkable difference for neighboring countries.

The U.S. firm that must distribute through large numbers of small retailers in a foreign market will find it a different challenge from the distribution task in the domestic market. Small retailers offer limited services to manufacturers who sell through them. They are short on both capital and space, which reduces the amount of inventory they can carry. For the manufacturer this limitation means a narrower line of products will be carried, and out-of-stock situations will be more frequent, both of which reduce sales. Small store size means less room for product display, which applies not only to shelf space, but also to point-of-purchase displays for which no space may be available. Small-scale retailing is generally weak and inefficient. Manufacturers can expect little contact, cooperation, or feedback. Because more direct distribution is usually not feasible, a pull strategy may be the best alternative.

Retail institutions are evolving around the world. Some developing countries are trying to improve the size and efficiency of retailers. For an idea of where certain countries stand, see Exhibit 6-3. Korea, for example, opened its first supermarkets in 1971. With government tax incentives, they expanded rapidly to more than 1,500 in the first decade. In western Europe, apart from Italy, the trend is to larger size, self-service, and more discounting—conditions familiar to U.S. marketers. These developments will lessen the differences between retail channels abroad and those in the United States. The internationalization of retailing will further that trend. Sears, K Mart and Toys'R'Us are some of the many U.S. retailers operating abroad. Meanwhile, the U.S. retailing market has been similarly invaded by Europeans. Such "American" stores as Brooks Brothers (Marks & Spencer) and A&P (Tengelmann) are European-owned.

As indicated in Exhibit 6-4, the use of scanning devices in stores is still quite low, even in highly developed markets. Without them, it is more difficult to track and plan inventory. The rapid pace of hardware and software improvements at ever-decreasing prices and the importance of relationship marketing and micromarketing will increase the adoption rate of new retail technologies.

EXHIBIT 6-3   *Size of Retailers in Selected Countries*

Country	Average Employment per Retailer
Colombia	1.6
Peru	1.9
Mexico	2.2
Taiwan	2.8
Netherlands	3.3
Japan	4.4
France	4.5
Australia	4.9
South Africa	6.6
Malaysia	7.7
Indonesia	11.2
United States	13.3
Germany	14.5

Source: *International Marketing Data and Statistics 1998*, 22nd ed. (London: Euromonitor Plc, 1998); *European Marketing Data and Statistics 1998*, 33rd ed. (London: Euromonitor Plc, 1998).

EXHIBIT 6-4   *Retail Technology: Number of Stores Using Scanning Devices*

Country	Number of Retail Outlets	Number of Stores Using Scanning Devices	Percent Using Scanners
Austria	33,200	3,490	10.51
Hong Kong	52,700	833	1.58
South Africa	60,400	688	1.13
Philippines	120,100	20	0.01
Australia	160,200	5,013	3.13
Chile	164,800	53	0.03
Greece	173,500	16	0.00
Colombia	445,500	8	0.00
South Korea	730,000	1,333	0.18
Brazil	760,000	81	0.01
Thailand	807,000	6	0.00
Mexico	899,300	372	0.04
United States	1,516,300	NA	NA
Japan	1,591,200	117,866	7.41
China	10,063,000	11	0.00

Source: *International Marketing Data and Statistics 1998*, 22nd ed. (London: Euromonitor Plc, 1998); *European Marketing Data and Statistics 1998*, 33rd ed. (London: Euromonitor Plc, 1998).

Nonstore Retailing

The many forms of nonstore retailing include vending machines, catalogs, home shopping television networks, and telemarketing. All are becoming more sophisticated as technology improves, but the type drawing the most attention now is the virtual store. The Internet and other online services that constitute interactive home shopping (IHS), provide instantaneous access to customers around the world. A recent IBM commercial popularized the idea that even small operations in a remote Italian village can market their products to Americans, Germans, and Japanese.

The English retailer, Coppernob replaced its High Street store with its "Virtual Catwalk," where animated models walk down a virtual runway and viewers can examine the fashions more closely by stopping the action and zooming in on a particular item. It is designed as a "worldwide showcase," but it also provides entertainment through its unique presentation of fashions, and by providing links to Internet sites that feature avant-garde music, video, and news at <http://www.virtual-catwalk.com>.

Although catalog sales are an important form of nonstore retailing, many retailers are using the latest technology to produce compact disc versions of their catalogs, and others are developing web pages. Both are more interactive than catalogs, and they can provide greater detail on command. Setup costs for comparable catalog, web page, or CD formats are likely to be similar, but web maintenance, and the reproduction and mailing charges for CDs are likely to be lower than the reproduction and mailing costs associated with a catalog.

Figures on usage are sketchy, but an estimated 100 million users found their way to the Internet in 1997. With the number doubling each year, the Internet may have more than 1 billion "surfers" worldwide by 2002. IHS sales estimates also vary wildly, with figures ranging from as little as $2.5 billion annually today, to forecasts of over $300 billion by 2000. By 2002 predictions have at least one-third of all computer software sales taking place online and online travel-related sales exceeding $12 billion. Arthur Andersen Consulting predicts $85 billion in electronic grocery shopping alone by 2007.

Business-to-business electronic commerce is expected to grow even more rapidly, accounting for nearly 10 percent of total sales by 2003 in the U.S. market—approximately $140 billion in e-commerce! These figures indicate that a word of warning is appropriate for those considering opening a virtual store—vendors may get more orders than they bargained for. When demand exceeds the capacity to supply merchandise, those merchants may lose customers who get tired of waiting for backorders.

Advantages and disadvantages come hand-in-hand with establishing a global presence on the Internet. A major advantage is, everyone can see you. A major disadvantage is, everyone can see you. The Internet provides a relatively cheap and quick way to increase the awareness of your company and its products. Yet, it is also possible to offend many people, or at least cause confusion for those who do not understand or speak the language used in your web pages. Exhibit 6-5 presents only a few of the issues to consider when constructing web pages.

Something else to consider: With 85 percent of Internet purchases taking place in North America in 1997, electronic commerce is not as global as perhaps believed. It is expected that only 10 percent of Europeans will be online by the year 2000. The European telecommunications industry is being deregulated, but the practice of charging for time spent on the

EXHIBIT 6-5   *Nonstore Retailing: The Internet*

Developing a Global Web Presence
1. Use simple language
2. Avoid complicated sentence structures
3. Use the active voice
4. Avoid humor
5. Use graphics to help communicate written concepts
6. Avoid complicated and unnecessary graphics

Source: Adapted from Morelli, Laura, "Writing for a Global Audience," *Marketing News* vol. 32, no. 17 (August 17, 1998), p. 16.

phone for local calls and the popularity of Minitel over the Internet in France have decreased e-commerce adoption rates in Europe. Even the lower prices of powerful personal computers (less than $500 for a complete system) still place them beyond the purchasing ability of a large portion of the world's population.

INTERNATIONAL PHYSICAL DISTRIBUTION

Physical distribution is the storage, handling, and moving of products from producer to customer. The cost of these activities in domestic marketing frequently amounts to one-fifth of the firm's sales. Considering these costs, physical distribution deserves careful management attention. For the same reason, complete books are devoted to the subject. In international marketing, physical distribution is even more costly and complicated. It has two dimensions: (1) physical distribution *within* each foreign market, and (2) distribution *across* national boundaries. In most of its foreign markets, the firm is not responsible for physical distribution of its products because its representative there, the distributor or licensee, takes care of it. This arrangement limits the management burden to those markets where the firm has marketing subsidiaries (or production and marketing subsidiaries).

In those markets where the firm is responsible for its physical distribution, its goal is the same as at home—minimizing costs while maintaining a high level of customer service. Although it is tempting to try to

BOX 6-2   *Vanity Fair's New Way to Serve Customers*

Vanity Fair Corporation (VF), maker of Lee and Wrangler jeans, JanSport backpacks, and Jantzen swimwear, devised their market response system (MRS) in the late 1980s. By implementing the newest hardware and software technologies over the next decade, the MRS evolved into a sophisticated system designed to replenish retail inventories more quickly and efficiently. Electronic data interchange (EDI) between VF and retailers assures replenishment of stock in a few days, rather than the few weeks it took before this system was implemented. Furthermore, by closely monitoring sales of specific styles, colors, and sizes in each store, VF is now able to practice micromarketing, which essentially allows tailoring of product assortments to every retail outlet. Everyone benefits from MRS. VF and retailers can maintain smaller inventories, and turnover at the retail level is brisk with few out-of-stock items or leftovers that must be marked down. If straight leg-jeans are hot items in London and embroidered shirts are selling well in Berlin, customers can be sure of getting the style, fit, and size they want every time they walk into a store.

Depending on the retailer's needs, the system can be highly automated. Product data that is scanned at the register, goes to strategically placed warehouses for immediate shipment. Inventory is also closely monitored at warehouses and when inventories for specific items go down, orders are sent directly to manufacturing centers around the globe. The cost savings associated with the EDI system allows VF to remain competitive, and the final consumer benefits by lower-priced products. Being able to track and analyze sales trends on a specific and small scale allows for better planning for VF and retailers. Because retail space is a precious commodity, manufacturers who can provide higher turnover and better profit margins, gain more preferential shelf space on the retail floor.

Source: Annual reports and company sources.

apply whatever logistical systems it uses at home, a firm will find some modifications are necessary to meet the differences in its foreign market situation. These differences are of two kinds. One is the position of the firm in the market. Where the firm is not producing locally but is importing from its plant in another country, its supply lines and inventories will be affected. Also, in most foreign markets, the firm's volume of business will be smaller and its product line narrower than at home, further constraining its logistical options. A second kind of foreign market difference is in the physical distribution infrastructure, such as warehousing and transportation media. In Europe, for example, river transport is important.

In Latin America, where mountains and jungles are found in many countries along with limited paved highways, air transport plays a major role.

> Pepsi-Cola provides an interesting example of the potential diversity of means of transportation. Pepsi claims to reach consumers abroad in many ways not used in the United States: "On foot. In baskets on bike handlebars. By airlift. On the heads of African women. By bus. By station wagon. Even by donkey."

Major Elements in International Physical Distribution

Moving goods across national boundaries introduces many complications. We do not have space for a major analysis of this subject, so we will identify and explain briefly the principal factors in the task of international physical distribution.

U.S. Export Restrictions

All countries regulate the movement of goods across their frontiers. For U.S. firms that means that most goods exported are regulated, and some permission or license is required before they can be shipped abroad. This regulation is not usually an onerous burden, except for strategic materials. Generally, the exporter must contact the Department of Commerce to make the necessary arrangements. For special products, some other government agency is authorized to give export permission. For example:

- Military equipment is licensed by the Department of State
- Atomic energy material is licensed by the Atomic Energy Commission
- Narcotic drugs are licensed by the Department of Justice
- Tobacco plants and tobacco seeds are licensed by the Department of Agriculture

Foreign Market Import Restrictions

Countries set up many different kinds of barriers to regulate the entry of foreign goods into their markets. The purpose of these barriers is usually to protect domestic producers from foreign competition, as in the requests of the United Auto Workers (UAW) for protection against Japanese car imports into the United States. The other side of the coin, of course, is that such barriers raise the price to domestic consumers. The two major import barriers are tariffs and quotas. A *tariff* is a special tax imposed on goods coming from another country. The tariff barrier may force the firm to adjust its price for that market, ship modified or unassembled products to get a lower rate, or, in the worst case, give up the market. Oftentimes, the firm may still be competitive after paying the tariff. Japanese cars, for example, pay less than 3 percent duty when shipped into the United States.

> Shenandoah Valley Poultry Company was shipping frozen poultry into Europe and fighting against a 40 percent tariff. Then, Shenandoah began seasoning its frozen turkey parts. Seasoned, the parts were classified as a prepared food in Germany and were then subject to a lower, 17 percent duty.

An *import quota* is a quantitative limit on the amount of imports, that is, so many pounds or units. The exporting firm may have to obtain an import license to have a share of the quota. If the quota is too restrictive, the only answer may be to produce inside the market—or give it up. For example, Japanese automakers moved into U.S. production to maintain their market share here.

Ocean Shipping and Insurance

Except for markets in Canada and Mexico, U.S. export markets generally require ocean shipping and insurance. Transoceanic shipment does not pose serious problems, but both ocean shipping and insurance will probably involve new companies and different kinds of contracts and operating methods from those used in domestic shipping. A different kind of experience and expertise is needed for international shipping, which is why firms often employ a foreign freight forwarder to handle the job.

Export Documentation

Because of the greater time and distance, the extra transportation and insurance required, and the fact that two political jurisdictions are involved, documentation for export is much greater than for domestic shipping. Two general kinds of documentation are required: first, *commercial* documents for shipping, forwarding, and insurance companies, and second, *government*-required documents, such as a shipper's export declaration, a consular invoice, or a certificate of origin. An average shipment can require more than 40 documents and several hundred copies. Documents are needed to leave the exporting country and to enter the importing country and for all those who will handle the merchandise in both countries. This paperwork is considered the most onerous task in exporting. It is not an unmanageable burden, however, as evidenced by the more than

100,000 U.S. firms successfully engaged in exporting. Of course, many firms pass on this burden through the use of the foreign freight forwarder.

The Foreign Freight Forwarder

Up to this point we have been discussing barriers and constraints to international physical distribution. Now, happily, we can mention an institution whose role is to ease the exporter's task. The full-service foreign freight forwarder can handle almost all paperwork, shipping, and insurance arrangements for the exporter. They are specialists in the mechanics of export trade. Because of their experience, expertise, and the economies they enjoy from serving many clients, foreign freight forwarders are used by many large exporters as well as by smaller firms.

Export Packing

Normal packing used for domestic shipments will rarely be suitable for export shipping because of the greater distances and increased potential for hazards inherent in export transportation methods. Consider the inland transportation in both the exporting and importing countries plus ocean shipping, which generally means more frequent and rougher handling, greater chances for pilferage, salt water exposure, climate changes, and so forth. These elements call for sturdier, more costly packing, which can raise freight charges and possibly even duties where they are assessed on gross weight. All these factors motivate a search for efficient export packing, perhaps with the aid of the freight forwarder. The same factors also make air cargo look more attractive because some of the problems noted are avoided when shipping by air.

Review of International Physical Distribution

We have noted just a few of the problems and complexities involved in international physical distribution. Special expertise is required to work in this area. In addition to developing company experience in managing this task, the international marketer will call on the expertise and assistance of such service organizations as the foreign freight forwarder, shipping lines, and marine insurance companies. In closing this section, we offer an example from Africa to show the importance of imagination and innovation in solving problems in international physical distribution.

Serving northern Nigeria was difficult for firms exporting to that country. Shipping in by sea via Lagos meant three months or longer en route and the probability of a lot of pilferage. Even air freight tended to set at Nigerian airports for a week or more and be subject to pilferage. To overcome these problems, European and Algerian trucking companies pioneered a route from the Mediterranean across the Sahara. A U.K. hauler noted, "We have been going across for two years without one claim for loss or damage." The route through Algeria is also quick—22 days from the United Kingdom through to Kano.

SUMMARY

We have looked at the three tasks in the management of distribution in international marketing. The first task is choosing a method of entry into foreign markets. The easiest and least expensive ways to enter foreign markets are by indirect exporting or by licensing a foreign producer. Direct exporting or producing abroad are more costly and difficult ways of entering foreign markets, but they may also lead to greater sales and profits. The choice of entry method is especially important because it strongly affects the rest of the firm's marketing program in foreign markets.

The second task is the management of distribution channels within the firm's foreign markets. This task is complicated by the uniqueness of each market's infrastructure and the distribution possibilities it offers the firm. The task is simplified, however, because the international marketer is responsible for local distribution only in those countries where the firm has a marketing subsidiary. In its other markets the firm's distribution will be handled by another party, such as a distributor or licensee.

The third task, international physical distribution, is hampered by greater distances, differing forms of transportation, and government requirements. Because of the complexity of this task, international marketers often leave much of the work to foreign freight forwarders who specialize in the mechanics of export trade.

We have considered the kinds of products we should offer to world markets (Chapter 5) and the ways to reach foreign customers with those products (Chapter 6). In Chapter 7, we shall consider how to price products for international markets.

QUESTIONS

1. Why is the choice of entry method into foreign markets such a critical decision?

2. Identify the varied ways a firm can reach foreign markets from domestic production sources.
3. What is the difference between indirect and direct exporting?
4. What are some of the factors that encourage firms to build factories abroad to serve foreign markets?
5. Discuss the advantages and disadvantages of joint ventures as a way of entering foreign markets.
6. In which of its foreign markets is the firm responsible for managing distribution channels? How does it deal with local distribution in its other markets?
7. What are some of the differences in retailing operations in world markets?
8. How is a firm's marketing in a country affected when it must sell through small retail outlets?
9. Identify the major elements in international physical distribution.
10. What is the role of the foreign freight forwarder?

FURTHER READING

1. Alba, Joseph W., John G. Lynch, Barton Weitz, Chris Janiszewski, Richard Lutz, Alan Sawyer, and Stacy Wood, "Interactive Home Shopping: Consumer, Retailer, and Manufacturer Incentives to Participate in Electronic Marketplaces," *Journal of Marketing* vol. 61, no. 3 (July 1997), pp. 38–53.
2. Bowles, Richard, "Food Retailing Takes Off," *China Business Review* vol. 25, no. 5 (September–October 1998), pp. 30–31.
3. Cateora, Philip R. and John L. Graham, *International Marketing*, 10th ed. (Boston, MA: Irwin/McGraw-Hill, 1999), Chapters 14 and 15.
4. Gosh, Shikhar, "Making Business Sense of the Internet," *Harvard Business Review*, (March–April 1998), p. 126.
5. Russow, Lloyd C. and Andrew Solocha, "A Review of the Screening Process within the Context of the Global Assessment Process," *Journal of Global Marketing* vol. 7, no. 1 (1993), pp. 65–85.
6. Terpstra, Vern, and Chou-Ming Yu, "Piggybacking: A Quick Road to Internationalization," *International Marketing Review* vol. 7, no. 4 (1990), p. 5.
7. Terpstra, Vern, and Ravi Sarathy, *International Marketing*, 7th ed. (Fort Worth, TX: Dryden Press, 1997), Chapters 10 and 11.

CHAPTER 7
International Dimensions
of Pricing

P rice is the variable in the marketing mix that most directly affects the firm's revenue—unit price times quantity sold equals the revenue coming into the firm. Therefore pricing is of interest to financial managers in addition to marketing managers. In international marketing, still other parties have an interest in the firm's prices such as customs and tax officials. Although pricing is a challenging job in domestic marketing, it is, not surprisingly, even more complex in international marketing.

Two major pricing tasks face the international marketer: *pricing for export*, and *pricing within foreign markets*. Export pricing involves the marketer *in the firm's home market* setting the price that will be paid by an intermediary (occasionally an ultimate customer) in the foreign market. It is cross-border pricing. Foreign market pricing involves the firm's marketer *in the foreign country* setting the price that will be paid by local buyers. It is foreign domestic pricing by the multinational firm. Thus these pricing situations differ on three dimensions: the locus of the decision (home country versus foreign market); the person making the decision (home office exporter/marketer versus foreign subsidiary marketer); and the constraints affecting the decision.

PRICING FOR EXPORT

A large part of international marketing involves the movement of goods across national boundaries, or exporting. A second major part of international marketing is the firm in a foreign market that sells goods produced in that country, which therefore do not cross national boundaries. Each of these international marketing tasks produces different pricing situations. We shall begin with exporting and identify the variables which affect pricing for export.

Objectives in Foreign Markets

Every activity the firm undertakes is presumably meant to help it achieve its objectives. The same is true of pricing. When it comes to export pricing, however, the situation is somewhat ambiguous. For one thing, the firm's goals or objectives in export markets may not be the same as in the domestic market. Furthermore, the firm's goals are likely to differ between export markets. These differences in objectives may result in different strategies in pricing between foreign and domestic markets and among different foreign markets themselves. Firms generally consider their domestic market as the primary one and have less ambitious goals for foreign markets as to sales volume, market share, and so forth. Pricing and marketing strategies will differ when foreign markets are perceived as being of secondary importance. In some firms, export markets are considered as important as the domestic market, and occasionally as even more critical to the firm's growth.

Firms not only have different objectives in foreign markets as compared with their home market, they often differentiate between export markets also. This behavior is not unreasonable. The French market, for example, with 58 million people and a per capita income over \$22,000 would most likely be more important to a firm than would a country perhaps like Bolivia, with only 8 million people and a per capita income of under \$4,000. Firms, therefore, have different objectives in export markets according to the market's potential importance to the firm. In large markets, they set more ambitious goals for volume of sales, market share, and width of product line. These goals, in turn, will affect their export pricing strategy.

Export Price or Domestic Price?

The appropriate question for the export manager to ask is, What is our profit maximizing price for each export market? (Assuming the firm's goal is profit maximization.) In more cases, however, the firm's discussion of export prices will begin with its domestic price, so it is worthwhile to consider the relation between the two. No presumptive reason dictates why the firm's ex-factory price, the price at the firm's loading dock for exports should be different from its ex-factory price for domestic sales. Nevertheless, export prices in companies fall into three categories: less than, equal to, and greater than the domestic price. What accounts for this diversity? Marketing texts indicate three main inputs to the pricing process an analysis of costs, a study of market demand, and a review of competitors' prices. Each of these can work to make export prices different from domestic. Let us look at each in turn.

Costs

Costs are important in pricing because the firm must cover its costs to survive. Many costs are allocated both to exports and to domestic sales, but the costs may differ according to the destination of the product. One would expect *production costs* to be the same for exports and the domestic market, but frequently it is not true. An export product that must be modified for the metric system, differences in electrical voltage, or otherwise altered could mean shorter production runs and higher costs. Conversely, if the product is sold as a simplified or stripped down version in export markets, production costs could be lower for exports. Allocation of *overhead and other costs* should be done according to the way the export and domestic products benefit from the outlay. Most *domestic marketing costs,* for example, should not be allocated to exports because exports receive no benefit from them. On the other hand, exports alone must pay for the operation of the export department.

Research and development costs are allocated entirely to domestic sales by many U.S. firms, making export costs lower. This practice is strongly opposed by the IRS, however, because R&D expenses are deducted against U.S. taxes and the U.S. government loses revenue to the extent that R&D costs are not recovered in the relevant export prices. Another consideration is that exports may require special extra *packing,* which would raise their cost. They will certainly require more *paperwork* than domestic sales. It is estimated that more than 60 hours are needed for documentation alone on the average export shipment and that such paperwork may equal as much as 10 percent of the value of goods shipped. Finally, varied *miscellaneous costs* are associated with exports. Export inventories or accounts receivable may be relatively higher than domestic because of the greater time and distance. Export credit losses may be different. (In fact, they are usually lower.) In today's world another cost is the risk associated with currency fluctuations if the firm quotes in foreign currencies.

Sound export pricing requires careful accounting to determine which costs are attributable to exports. By themselves, these costs could lead to export prices either higher or lower than domestic prices.

Market Demand

Even more important than costs in setting prices is what the market is able and willing to pay. That in turn is determined by how much consumers like the product and what their income is. Even with low-income consumers, an intense demand can sell products at high prices, such as a drug addict buying a fix, or a teenager paying $80 for a pair of Levis in Moscow. Few export marketers face such intense demand for their products, however, so ability to pay is important. Ability to pay is essentially a function of the income level of the consumer. One indicator of ability to pay is per capita income (per capita GNP). Per capita income varies widely around the world. Because this particular measure is merely an average, however, care must be taken to include other measures of wealth distribution. For U.S. exporters, most foreign markets have a lesser ability to pay than the domestic market. By itself, this lesser ability to pay would suggest that an export price lower than the domestic price is desirable in most countries. When profitability of a product can't be achieved by pricing alone, product modification may help: smaller sizes, fewer features, simplification, and an emphasis on utility rather than luxury.

Competition

Practicing marketers are well aware of the constraints competition sets on their pricing freedom. The firm usually has to conform more or less to the going market price. In markets with a small number of competitors, the firm may have more freedom in setting prices, although oligopolists can also exert a lot of pressure on competitors' prices, as when auto manufacturers follow each other's rebate programs. In export pricing the same competitive pressures exist. The main difference lies in the fact that in each export market the firm faces a different competitive situation as to the number of competitors, their size and strength, and their pricing strategies. In countries where there are deeply entrenched competitors the exporter may have to accept the going price, or perhaps even go under the current price to break into the market.

An auto executive disliked selling in the French market against Renault, because Renault is a government-owned firm. Their primary goal is to maintain employment rather than to maximize profits. For this reason they are willing to accept a lower price, which forces competitors to keep their prices at an unprofitable level. In Germany, on the other hand, the auto companies are interested in making profits and so allow competitors to set more profitable prices.

In some export markets, the firm may have little competition, especially if it is the first with a product in that market. In such countries, the firm may be able to charge a higher price than it gets in its more competitive home market. The impact of competition within differing competitive situations in export markets may indicate appropriate export prices either higher or lower than at home.

Dumping

We have noted certain situations in which the appropriate price for an export market may be lower than the price in the home market. Such a price may be profit maximizing for the firm and pleasing to foreign customers. This practice is technically known as dumping, however, and may lead to complaints by local competitors, as with U.S. firms' complaints against various Asian manufacturers. These complaints in turn may lead to foreign government action against the exporter. In this way, an export pricing strategy that is otherwise desirable may be frustrated. It should be noted, however, that this practice, with the unhappy name of dumping, can be employed in those markets that have no local producers. Because the customers are happy with these prices, no one complains to the government.

Computers are getting cheaper every day. A contributing factor is ever-cheaper DRAM (Dynamic Random Access Memory) chips, which reportedly decreased in price by 45 percent in 1996, another 75 percent in 1997, and yet another 60 percent a year later! In early 1998, Texas Instruments sold its memory operations to the last remaining U.S. DRAM producer, Micron Technology. Only a few months later, Micron filed a petition with the U.S. Department of Commerce and the International Trade Commission charging Taiwanese producers with dumping—selling chips at prices below what it cost to manufacture these DRAM chips. Rather than basing sales prices on total cost, a variable cost pricing strategy can be used to gain market share, a strategy some have chosen to adopt. Yet, earlier in the decade, Korean chip manufacturers Hyundai and LG Semicon were also charged with dumping. Both are now paying U.S.-proscribed countervailing duties, imposed to increase market prices for these manufacturers. Micron hoped similar action would be taken against their Taiwanese competitors.[1]

---

[1]Louise Kehoe, "Taiwan: Chip Producers Accused of U.S. Dumping," *Financial Times* (October 26, 1998) <http://www.ft.com>.

Price Escalation in Exporting

The physical and economic distance between the producer and the ultimate consumer is usually much greater in exporting than in the domestic market. This extra distance means that more transportation and insurance services will be required as well as a longer distribution channel with more intermediaries. Furthermore, additional charges for export documentation and import duties are a reality of exporting. All these things add up to the phenomenon known as price escalation in exporting. Export price escalation refers to the significant increase in the price of the product as it passes through the many steps from exporter to final consumer. Because exporting usually requires several more steps and because each step involves a cost, the final consumer price in export markets is often much higher than in the domestic market. This price escalation can best be shown by Exhibit 7-1, which indicates some of the extra steps and their charges associated in exporting. The importer/distributor has a higher margin than the wholesaler because of the extra work in clearing the imported goods.

The particular figures and assumptions used in Exhibit 7-1 result in an export price almost 50 percent higher than the final consumer price in the

EXHIBIT 7-1   *Export Price Escalation*

	Domestic Sale	Export Sale
Factory Price	$7.50	$7.50
Domestic Freight	0.70	0.70
	8.20	8.20
Export Documentation		0.50
		8.70
Ocean Freight & Insurance		1.20
		9.90
Import Duty (12% of landed cost)		1.19
		11.09
Wholesaler Markup (15%)	1.23	
	9.43	
Importer/Distributor Markup (22%)		2.44
		13.53
Retail Markup (50%)	4.72	6.77
Final Consumer Price	**$14.15**	**$20.30**

domestic market. Of course, other cases can be cited in which the price escalation is less than in our example. However, just as likely are cases in which export price escalation is greater than shown in Exhibit 7-1. Whenever export price escalation does occur, it becomes difficult or impossible for the firm to realize a lower price in the foreign market than at home—a goal which is sometimes desirable as previously mentioned. Price escalation may be large enough to make the firm's product noncompetitive in some export markets. In trying to overcome the problems of price escalation, the firm can consider several possible strategies:

1. Shipping modified or unassembled products to lower transportation costs and duties
2. Lowering its export price at the factory, thus reducing the multiplier effect of all the markups
3. Changing its freight and/or duty classifications for a possible lowering of these costs
4. Producing within the export market to eliminate the extra steps

We do not have space to discuss these strategies individually, but we must at least note that the firm does have alternatives to staying out of the market when faced with the problem of export price escalation.

The Choice of Currency for Export Price Quotes

In setting export prices, firms face a problem with no counterpart in their domestic experience: they must not only set prices, but also decide in which currency those prices shall be quoted. U.S. firms are accustomed to transacting all of their business in U.S. dollars. In exporting they deal with customers who are accustomed to handling all their business in their own domestic currencies—francs, yen, pesos, and so on. In an international transaction such as exporting, whose currency should be used? If the U.S. dollar had a fixed relationship to these other currencies, exporters would have no problem. If the U.S. dollar always equaled 10 rupees, 200 yen, or 0.5 pounds sterling, for example, then it would be simple arithmetic to translate a dollar price into some other currency. However, in today's world of floating exchange rates, the value of other currencies in terms of the dollar is constantly fluctuating. Indeed it may fluctuate several percent in a single day. Two brief examples illustrate the problems this currency fluctuation can pose.

Unicorp, a capital equipment manufacturer, won a bid for an installation priced at U.S. $1 million or 80 million Latinian pesos as of January 5, the date the contract was awarded. The price was quoted in pesos. Because of the time required for production, shipping, installation, and normal credit terms, the account was paid to Unicorp—80 million pesos—on July 1. During that six month period, the value of the peso vis à vis the U.S. dollar had declined by 18 percent, so 80 million pesos now equaled only $820,000 instead of $1 million. If Unicorp had quoted a dollar price, they would have received the $1 million. The customer, however, would have had to pay 97,560,975 pesos instead of the 80 million agreed to.

CBC received a $100,000 (or 85,500 euros) order from Germany on January 1. Normal processing, shipping, and credit terms meant that payment of $100,000 was received on March 1 (the quote was in dollars). The German exporter had to pay only 76,950 euros for the $100,000, however, because the euro had appreciated 10 percent against the dollar in that 60 days. If CBC had quoted that order in euros, they would have received the benefit of the change in the exchange rate, for the euros on May 10 was worth $110,000 instead of $100,000.

Given the uncertainty in international transactions under floating exchange rates, the firm must exercise great care in the choice of a currency (or currencies) for export price quotes. We shall review the considerations involved in choosing a currency from the viewpoint of the U.S. exporter. Two basic alternatives are available: to quote in U.S. dollars or to quote in customers' currencies. Quoting in dollars is the preferred practice of U.S. exporters because of several advantages. It simplifies pricing and record keeping between domestic and foreign sales, and between foreign markets. All get uniform treatment. It eliminates exchange risk for the exporter who then has no position (neither short nor long) in a foreign currency. The firm conducts business in dollars and knows exactly how many dollars will be received when the account is paid, whenever that may be. Eliminating the exchange risk allows the exporter to extend longer credit terms because the firm need not fear an exchange loss such as Unicorp experienced. The major drawback to quoting in the exporter's currency is that it puts all the exchange risk on the buyer, and the competitive situation may not permit it.

Quoting export prices in customers' currencies is a more marketing-oriented approach to price. Customers prefer dealing in their own currency just as the exporter does. It simplifies their business and facilitates price comparisons between their domestic and foreign suppliers. Most importantly, it saves them from the risk of exchange loss since they then have no position in a foreign currency. When the buyer has a choice of several suppliers, they will choose one that spares them the foreign exchange risk, all else being equal. Frequently, then, the exporter will find it necessary to quote in the customers' currencies.

Various protective measures can be considered by the exporter who faces exchange risk. One is hedging its open position in the forward exchange market. Because it will receive a given amount of foreign currency at a specified future date, a firm can sell short the same amount of foreign currency to be delivered at the same date. That hedges or covers the open position and eliminates the uncertainty. Alternatively, exporters may lessen their risk by extending credit for a shorter period of time, say 30 days instead of 60 days. While this method does not eliminate the risk, it does limit its extent. Finally, the exporter may try to insert an escalation clause in the sales contract to protect itself against exchange rate fluctuations. The competitive situation will be a major factor determining the feasibility of such a clause.

Export Price Quotations

Export price quotations are complex and technical, and details about them are beyond the scope of this text. However, because they are part of the sales contract and because they spell out certain responsibilities of buyer and seller and specify when the title to the goods changes hands, some appreciation of their nature is necessary. We shall look at four examples of the many different export price quotations.

1. *Ex-Factory.* An ex-factory contract means that the buyer takes possession of the merchandise at the factory of the seller and bears all risks and expenses from there on. This practice limits the exporter's risks and responsibilities, but places a great burden on the foreign buyer. It is not a recommended price quotation except when dealing with large foreign buyers who have representation in the exporter's country, such as a Japanese trading company, for example.
2. *F.O.B. (free on board) named inland carrier.* This type of quotation is not much different from an ex-factory quote. The seller has the merchandise loaded on a train or truck outside its factory. From the marketing viewpoint, it has the same shortcomings as the ex-factory quote. Nevertheless, it is a popular price quotation with U.S. exporters because they use it domestically and because it limits their responsibility.
3. *F.A.S. (free along side) vessel, named port of shipment.* With an F.A.S. quotation, the exporter maintains ownership of the goods and responsibility for their handling until they are placed alongside the ship at

the port of embarkation. In this quotation the exporter has greater risk (owning the goods for a longer time) and greater responsibility (arranging inland transportation in its own country), but it lessens the burden on the foreign buyer. The F.A.S. quote is higher than the F.O.B. quote because inland freight is included.

4. *C.I.F. (cost, insurance, freight) named port of destination.* A C.I.F. quote transfers title to the buyer once the merchandise is loaded aboard the ship or plane. However, the exporter assumes responsibility for arranging for and paying for transportation and insurance all the way to the foreign port. This practice means more work for the exporter but greater convenience for the foreign buyer. The C.I.F. quote is higher than others, of course, because it includes shipping and insurance.

Any of the export price quotations might be appropriate given the right circumstances. Normally, however, the C.I.F. quotation is considered the marketing-oriented approach. It is most convenient for the foreign buyer and also allows the buyer to compare the prices of domestic and foreign suppliers more easily. Foreign buyers have often complained about U.S. exporters' frequent use of F.O.B. pricing. It must be noted that the net amount received by the exporter is the same in all price quotations. Regardless of the price quotation used, the buyer will ultimately pay for all the shipping, handling, and insurance even if the exporter makes the arrangements for them. The differences between the quotes are in *when title passes*—and therefore the risks of ownership—and in *who is responsible for the arrangements* for shipping and insurance. The most efficient arrangement seems to be for each party to deal with nationals in its own country, as in a C.I.F. quote, which minimizes communications problems and allows each to deal in a familiar environment.

Exporting to Company Subsidiaries Abroad

Our discussion heretofore has considered the pricing of exports only to independent foreign buyers. When the firm is exporting to its own subsidiaries abroad, the pricing situation is quite different. Prices to subsidiaries could be lower or higher than those charged to independent buyers, depending on company objectives. Transfer pricing of goods exchanged within the corporate family is a complex technical and legal subject. We shall look at the topic briefly by noting the considerations involved in two kinds of transfer pricing situations: pricing at lower than arm's-length prices, and pricing at higher than arm's-length prices. (Arm's-length prices are those charged to independent buyers.)

Transfer Prices Lower Than Arm's-Length Prices

Three main reasons explain why the firm might desire to sell to its foreign subsidiaries at relatively low prices. One is to lessen the *impact of high duties.* A lower transfer price may allow the firm to be competitive in spite of the high duty. Because it owns the subsidiary, any profits from this strategy redound to the company. This strategy does not work when the firm lowers the price to an independent distributor. Another reason for a lower price is to enable the subsidiary to *enter a market* against tough competition, when the subsidiary is a profit center needing to show adequate returns. The third reason tempting a firm to charge lower prices to a subsidiary abroad is the *lower income tax rate* that exists in some countries. The lower price allows more income to be made in a lower tax jurisdiction, and that income is not subject to the higher U.S. tax rate until it is remitted back to the United States.

Even though low transfer prices to foreign subsidiaries may occasionally be a desirable strategy, such an approach has two major barriers. One is the foreign *customs office.* Countries put tariffs on imported goods to protect their own industries. If customs officials feel that exporters are trying to evade their tariff by artificially lowering prices, they are apt to retaliate by raising the stated price for purposes of assessing the duty. The second constraint on low transfer prices abroad is the U.S. Internal Revenue Service (IRS). Low transfer prices mean that more of the firm's income is earned in the foreign country at the expense of U.S. tax revenues. The IRS has authority to look at a firm's transfer prices and will challenge those prices it thinks are too low. The IRS prefers arm's-length prices, of course.

Transfer Prices Higher Than Arm's-Length Prices

Two situations might encourage a firm to transfer merchandise to its foreign subsidiary at a higher than arm's-length price. One is a *high corporate income tax rate* in the foreign country. If the importing country has a higher tax rate than the exporting country, the exporter would naturally prefer to make (or declare) its income at home to save on its total tax bill. The second situation encouraging high transfer prices is host country *restrictions on dividend repatriation.* Many countries are short of foreign exchange so they try to limit its use to high-priority items, usually necessary imports. Using their scarce foreign currencies to enable companies to repatriate profits is not a high-priority item. If an exporter has no other way to get profits out of such a country, the exporter is tempted to try to do it through high transfer prices to its subsidiary there. High transfer prices do not disturb either the IRS or foreign customs officials. They do, however, greatly disturb foreign tax authorities who are ever suspicious of multinationals' transfer prices and make every effort to police them. It is interesting to note that foreign customs officials and foreign tax authorities often take opposite positions on transfer prices.

PRICING WITHIN FOREIGN MARKETS

Only multinationals face the problems of setting prices *within* foreign markets, and then only in those countries where they have production and/or marketing subsidiaries. For example, see Box 7-1. As noted earlier, in countries where the firm is represented by distributors or licensees, these intermediaries handle the pricing for their markets. Foreign market pricing is still an important issue for multinationals, however, because the countries where they have their own subsidiaries are usually their largest, most important markets, accounting for the bulk of foreign sales and profits.

Variables in Foreign Market Pricing

Pricing for a foreign market is essentially *domestic* pricing within a foreign country. As such, the pricing tasks and situations are similar to those encountered in the firm's home market, such as new product pricing or product line pricing. Because these topics are covered in basic marketing texts, we shall limit ourselves to an overview of the international dimensions of foreign market pricing. Pricing within foreign markets differs from pricing in the home market simply because it is done in foreign countries where the parameters are different. Exhibit 7-2 lists the major variables affecting pricing within foreign markets. We shall discuss the impact of some of these variables on the firm's pricing strategies in foreign markets. Except for tariffs, the variables in Exhibit 7-2 are the same as in the domestic market. The important point, however, is that their values are usually different in each foreign market.

Company Goals

As we indicated in our discussion of export pricing, company goals often vary from country to country. This variation will be true in subsidiary markets as well as in export markets. In growth economies, the firm is more likely to stress maintenance or growth of market share. A penetration pric-

BOX 7-1   *Pricing in India*

Massachusetts-based Reebok had high expectations for its entry into India in 1995. With nearly 1 billion people and a rapidly growing middle class, Reebok planned to market its premium lines of sport shoes, including the new DMX 2000 running shoes, priced at nearly $125 per pair.

India is a competitive market. Reebok competes directly with other multi-nationals such as Nike, Adidas, and Bata India, and faces local challengers such as Action, Liberty, and Mesco's that typically sell lower-priced shoes. In 1997, Reebok sold only 250,000 pairs of shoes in India, compared with 300,000 pairs per day worldwide. After two years of dismal sales, *all* the multinationals revised their pricing strategies. They began focusing on marketing shoes in the $28 to $42 price range, because they learned that the Indian consumer was reluctant to spend $50 or more for fancy, high-priced footwear. Although discouraged, Reebok is projecting that they will break even for the first time in their 1998–1999 fiscal year.

Source: *Advertising Age, International Daily,* "Reebok Tries to Get It Right This Time in India"; "Reebok India Launch at Odds with Low-Price Strategy" (September 18, 1997); "Reebok India Claims Marketing Revamp Has Worked" (August 8, 1997).

ing strategy would be appropriate for that goal. In slow growth or stagnating economies, the firm might wish to maintain the status quo or treat the market as a "cash cow," adopting a pricing strategy appropriate to that goal. The initial variation in company objectives by country results largely from the variation in the economic, political, and legal environments in

EXHIBIT 7-2   *Variables Affecting Foreign Market Pricing*

Company Goals

Costs $\left\{ \begin{array}{l} \text{Manufacturing} \\ \text{Transportation} \\ \text{Marketing} \end{array} \right.$

Demand
Competition
Government Regulations
Taxes and Tariffs
Inflation
Product Line
Distribution Channels
Marketing Mix

host countries. As these environments change over time—with the introduction of the Euro, or the Asian financial crisis, for example—the firm's goals for that country will also change, leading to a modification of pricing strategies and tactics.

Costs

The multinational firm often has cost advantages over a domestic firm in a foreign market. As to *production costs,* the multinational may be a more efficient manufacturer and/or enjoy economies of scale enabling the firm to be especially price competitive. Furthermore, the multinational often has the option of supplying a market from a plant within the country or from one outside the country. Because plants in different countries have different cost structures and capacity availability, this flexibility can be an important pricing advantage.

> Retailers have been hard hit by the recession that made its way through Asia in 1998. The Muji ("no brand") retail chain in Japan, however is posting record profits. Value-conscious consumers are turning away from the higher-priced retailers like Daiei and Seibu. Pricing in Muji's 248 stores reflect the efficient manufacturing and distribution networks developed by the head of the company, Mr. Kaoru Ariga. While the products are designed in Japan for its Japanese customers, in order to keep costs low, they are typically of simple design and offered in few colors, and most are manufactured in China.[2]

Marketing costs included in a product price vary between subsidiaries for several reasons. One is that the costs of marketing services differ from country to country in marketing research, advertising, and distribution. Second, the firm's volume of business and width of product line differ among its subsidiaries. Most marketing activities lend themselves to economies of scale, so products in countries with smaller sales and narrower product lines may bear a heavier marketing cost component in their price. We saw in the chapter on distribution how a narrow product line led to unprofitable operations for General Foods in Japan and how they were forced to join with a large Japanese firm to realize the necessary marketing economies of scale. A third reason for international variation in the firm's marketing costs is that the firm's marketing mix will vary by country. The subsidiaries' relative reliance on price, advertising, personal sell-

---

[2]"Muji: Japanese Retailer Blooms in Recession," *Financial Times* (October 1, 1998).

ing, product quality, etc., is dependent on their situations and influences which marketing approaches they choose to use.

In the United States, Procter & Gamble uses television advertising as their major marketing tool—a pull strategy. In foreign countries without commercial TV, P&G must adapt its marketing mix to emphasize other methods to win the consumer. In countries with low labor costs such as India and Mexico, firms may use a push strategy employing hundreds of people in their salesforce, often on foot, bike, or public transportation.

Government Regulations

In the U.S. market, marketers must contend with pricing laws which include the Robinson-Patman Act. This law prohibits manufacturer price discrimination between wholesalers and/or retailers that cannot be justified on the basis of cost differences. This law has no counterpart in other countries, so the role of government in pricing abroad is of a different nature than in the United States. We should note, however, that although other countries have no Robinson-Patman-type laws, their governments occasionally challenge the firm's discounts to intermediaries, especially in the developed countries.

Danish antitrust authorities charged the managing director of Danish Unilever, Inc., with distributing more than $10 million in trade discounts to retailers in a campaign to grab a larger share of the Danish margarine market. Trade discounts are not illegal in Denmark, but the charge was that these discounts went beyond fair competition and that Unilever had failed to notify the registrar of restrictive trade practices whose approval is needed for unusual trade discounts.

The major role of governments in pricing abroad, however, is not the kind cited in the preceding Unilever example. Rather, it is government price controls. Many governments around the world have price controls in varying degrees, both in developed and developing countries. For example, some of the western European countries with price controls on manufacturers at one time included Belgium, France, Ireland, the Netherlands, Spain, Sweden, and the United Kingdom. The method of controlling prices usually follows this pattern: the manufacturer must apply for a price increase with data to support the request (increased wages, materials costs, etc.); after a required waiting period, the price can be increased *if* the request is approved. The waiting period was one month in Sweden and three months in Belgium, for example.

These controls pose two problems for firms. One is the arbitrary limit to the size of a price increase. This limit is usually a fixed percentage (in France one year it was 5 percent) or a percentage of the firm's increase in costs. In the United Kingdom, for example, the firm could recoup 100 percent of increased fringe benefits, but only two-thirds of increased wage costs. Firms complain that the rate of increase allowed is usually below their own rate of cost increase and rate of inflation. The major problem, however, is that the request for a price increase may be denied, a somewhat common occurrence. If a firm is regularly denied price increases, eventually its survival will be jeopardized. The following example is given, not as a typical case, but as a worst-case scenario.

> Gerber Products Co. had been operating in Venezuela since 1960. Unprofitable operations forced the firm to sell out in 1979. The company blamed price controls as a major factor in losses. Some of Gerber's products were still being sold at prices set in 1968. The government had refused repeated requests for price increases. The price squeeze forced Gerber to cut output from 88 varieties to as low as 12. The company reportedly lost $500,000 in the first six months of 1979. Not surprisingly, the new Venezuelan owners expected better treatment from their government.

Price controls may affect all kinds of products. Frequently, however, some products are considered more sensitive than others and are more likely to be subject to government control. Pharmaceuticals are a favorite target, and their prices are often controlled even in countries that don't normally control other prices. Countries in the Middle East, for example, are extremely strict on drug prices. Most Middle Eastern health ministries monitor prices throughout the region and also review a monthly British publication that lists drug prices in the United Kingdom, a country with a reputation for stringent control of pharmaceutical pricing. Beyond pharmaceuticals, foodstuffs are most commonly controlled, along with whatever products are considered essential and sensitive to consumers and, therefore, to politicians. The case of Mexico is illustrative. At one time, Mexico reduced its list of products under price controls from 274 to 64. The categories still controlled included foodstuffs, basic industrial products, essential raw materials, and products of important domestic industries including cigarettes, soaps, detergents, toothpaste, medicines, baby foods, home appliances, bottles and jars, trucks, buses, tractors, cardboard, and food packing materials.

The next section highlights some suggestions for dealing with government price controls because inflation and price controls often go together.

Inflation

U.S. firms have not had much experience with double-digit inflation in recent years. The experience is rare enough that U.S. marketing books have not given much attention to inflation in their discussion of pricing. Inflation in the United States is moderate compared to many high-inflation countries in the world economy. At one extreme, for example, the purchasing power of currencies in Argentina, Brazil, and Indonesia declined to less than one percent of their value. Brazil's inflation rates have fallen dramatically from over 1,000 percent in 1992, 1993, and 1994 to between 15 and 20 percent. In the mid 1990s, Russia had annual inflation rates over 100 percent, and Turkey experienced rates as high as 80 percent. Countries with transitional economies, including Hungary, Romania, and Turkmenistan have double-digit inflation rates, and Bulgaria's inflation rate reached nearly 100 percent recently. Exhibit 7-3 shows the differences in inflation rates between selected groups of countries. Because the

EXHIBIT 7-3   *Inflation in Selected Countries*

Lower Inflation Country	Annual Rate 1996	Higher Inflation Country	Annual Rate 1996
Ethiopia	−5.1%	Congo	657.4%
Bahrain	−0.2%	Venezuela	99.9%
Japan	0.1%	Turkey	80.4%
Saudi Arabia	1.2%	Guinea-Bissau	50.7%
Singapore	1.4%	Zambia	46.3%
Germany	1.5%	Malawi	37.6%
Netherlands	2.1%	Mexico	34.4%
United Kingdom	2.5%	Nigeria	29.3%
United States	2.9%	Iran	28.9%
Portugal	3.1%	Jamaica	26.4%
Malaysia	3.5%	Ecuador	24.4%
Italy	4.0%	Hungary	23.5%

Source: *World Development Indicators 1998, CD-ROM*, The International Bank for Reconstruction and Development/World Bank.

right-hand set of countries have inflation rates many times as high as those in the first column, they pose a pricing challenge to the marketing manager different from countries with moderate inflation rates.

Although it is interesting to note that inflation rates vary dramatically around the world, what are the implications for the firm's pricing in foreign markets? How do firms survive and prosper in high-inflation economies? Without price controls, pricing involves essentially *raising prices frequently* enough to keep up with inflation. Of course, the firm must watch competitors so as not to get too far above their prices. Good accounting is important also because the various cost components will have different inflation rates. The inflation rates for labor, raw materials, overhead, packaging, and transportation will all be different, so it is not sufficient to apply a general inflation rate in calculating the firm's costs and prices. Indeed, it would be most unusual if the firm's cost inflation rate were the same as the general inflation rate for the whole economy.

> To keep pace with Peru's rapid inflation, Procter & Gamble's Peruvian subsidiary had to raise detergent prices 20–30 percent every two weeks. In addition, P&G stopped providing 60-day free credit. It reduced credit to only 15–30 days with the cost split between the retailers and P&G.

The most serious problem of pricing in inflationary economies arises when inflation is coupled with government price controls, which is not uncommon. Because the firm can't raise prices without permission, *good cost accounting* is even more important to enable the firm to justify its request for a price increase. The multinationals might also wish to approach the price authorities along with the national trade association or competitors. The multinational may have a more sophisticated accounting system than national firms and be more able to justify a request for a price increase. However, it is unlikely that a multinational would be granted price increases quicker than or greater than those given to national firms. For this reason, the multinational might work with national firms in requesting increases.

Another approach to dealing with the combined problems of inflation and price controls is to *change the mix* of inputs used by the firm. If wage rates are rising at a faster rate than other costs, the firm might consider a more capital intensive production, as has happened in the U.S. and Japanese auto industries. If some raw materials or inputs are rising rapidly in price, the firm should seek inputs with more stable price behavior. Another alternative is to evaluate and *adjust the line of products* offered by the firm. Two reasons support this approach. One is that not all products are subject to the same degree of price controls. Where firms have the option, they try to move from price-controlled products to those that aren't controlled. The second reason is that not all products experience the same degree of cost inflation. Some use inputs with more stable costs, and the firm should consider such products as part of its offering. A final alternative is to *withdraw from the market.* This option is never desirable but may be necessary in extreme cases, as shown by the Gerber example.

Other Variables

Several other uncontrollable factors vary from one subsidiary market to another. *Demand* and *competition* were discussed under export pricing, but marketing managers in subsidiaries will have to give even closer attention to these market forces. Subsidiary marketers are immediately involved with local demand and competition in contrast to the export marketer who is one or two steps removed from the foreign market. *Product or sales taxes* vary from country to country and will affect the firm's prices. In the European Union, for example, member countries all have a value-added tax (similar to a sales tax). The tax rate differs between member countries, as well as between product categories—from 20 percent in Finland to zero in Belgium for some goods. Culture and changing habits also have an impact on pricing as the following example shows.

> Studies revealed that U.K. grocery shoppers were spending less time "doing their weekly shop." Because purchase decisions were being made in less time, manufacturers either had to influence the consumer in less time or develop long-term brand loyalty. Proctor & Gamble introduced "Every Day Low Pricing" (EDLP) pricing strategy in 1996 to instill a sense of sustained value, rather than rely on sales promotion, which tended to lead to short-term brand switching and seriously affected production schedules. By February 1997, however, after sales showed little or no growth in volume (perhaps because other leading manufacturers lowered their prices too), prices for most products were being raised to pre-EDLP levels. Therefore, the moral of the story is that if products are similar in the eyes of consumers, except for price, and the industry is dominated by a few large companies who can afford protracted price wars, discounting strategies do not always work well.[3]

---

[3]Cathy Bond, "P&G's Gamble: Price or Promotion?" *Marketing* (February 13, 1997).

All nations protect their home market, usually with *tariffs* on imported goods. Tariffs can have two different impacts on the firm's pricing. The most obvious impact is when the subsidiary is importing products for the local market and paying the duty on top of the transfer price. Even where the subsidiary is selling only locally made products, the tariff can still be a factor in that it helps to keep out low-priced competitors from other countries, giving more pricing freedom to the subsidiary. Finally, *distribution costs* are different from one country to another. One reason is that intermediary margins vary internationally and using similar channels may not mean similar costs. A second reason is that because of the country's distribution infrastructure or the firm's product line variability, the firm may be using different distribution channels in different markets.

EUROPEAN MONETARY UNION

European Monetary Union (EMU) includes the introduction of the euro, which is a new medium of exchange, a new currency. Introduction of the euro will have an impact on pricing for export as well as pricing within the European Union.

In May 1998, the European Union established semi-fixed exchange rates between the national currencies of the 11 EMU participants and the euro. "First-wave" countries include all EU members except the United Kingdom, and Denmark, which opted out, and Sweden and Greece because they could not meet the required criteria. On January 1, 1999, savings and investment instruments, insurance policies, government accounting and other statements were denominated in euros. During a three-year period, between January 1, 1999 and December 31, 2001 many items will be priced in two currencies, the national currency and euro. The national currencies will be removed from circulation between January 1, 2002 and June 30, 2002.

What is the impact for businesses operating in the EMU countries? In general, opportunities and competition increase, while operating costs and other expenses decrease. The many benefits include no exchange risks among euro participants and therefore fewer costs (e.g., forward contracts become unnecessary). As EMU proceeds, interest, inflation, and unemployment rates will converge across Europe. Pricing strategies can be more uniform and, because prices are denominated in the same currency and pricing policies are more similar, measuring performance becomes easier, allowing for easier comparison between subsidiaries.

On the other hand, added costs and other drawbacks include the need to restate prices on everything from menus to packages, advertisements, loans, and other agreements. Companies will have to list prices in euros and in the national currency for at least six months. Until now, national currency boundaries allowed companies to segment the market and charge different prices in each country. A recent EU Commission study showed that prices between the United Kingdom and Ireland differ by 40 percent in some cases. Other studies reveal that drug prices differ by as much as 300 percent across Europe; Big Macs cost 20 percent less in Spain than Belgium; bank charges vary by 60 percent and telephone calls by 25 percent across the EU. The practice of setting different prices in

BOX 7-2   *Euro's Impact on Tourists and European Citizens*

The euro promises benefits and drawbacks to consumers as well. Overall, products will be cheaper and prices more stable, but only after an initial period of confusion.

Benefits:
- People would be able to travel from one end of Europe to the other without having to exchange Spanish pesetas for Belgian francs. Depending on the service charges, a tourist typically lost between 25 and 50 percent when they had to stop in each EU country and exchange some of their money.
- Pricing would become more transparent. Formerly, if one could buy a Sony 27" television in the United Kingdom for 547 £ and the same television cost 1,443 DM in Germany, the consumer might not notice a price difference (at an exchange rate of 2.3 DM for 1 £, the TV costs about 80 £ more in Germany). But, if both countries used the euro, a 40–50 euro price difference might cause some consumers to purchase the product in one country over another.

Drawbacks:
- Imagine dealing with a foreign currency in your own country. People will need calculators with a euro button, much as it has a square root button, to enter the amount of a specific currency, press the button, and display the amount in euros.
- Small stores, street vendors, and some die-hard nationalists may only accept the national currency during the changeover period. Not only will the Europeans have to make sure they have enough cash when they leave home in the morning, they'll need enough of both euros and the national currency.

each market, or "pricing to market" will be more difficult because price differences will be transparent, or more obvious, to consumers since the products will all be priced in euros. Yet other practices are expected to continue, such as French government conventions with pharmaceutical companies and British price maintenance practices, which are likely to blunt some of the expected price convergence. As manufacturing facilities and warehouses are consolidated to cut costs in this competitive environment, shipping charges will differ from place to place. Demand for wine is higher in Spain, Italy, and France, while more beer is consumed in England, Germany, and Belgium. As we have discussed, demand, competition, and cost variations have substantial impact on pricing strategy, and contribute to ongoing price differences among the EMU countries.

SUMMARY

We have noted some of the major factors causing export pricing to be a different task from pricing to domestic customers. Export pricing is pricing to get goods *into* a foreign market. It usually means selling to foreign distributors or licensees who are then responsible for pricing the goods in their own country.

Pricing within foreign markets is similar to the task in the domestic market, so the firm can apply its domestic experience to some extent. Nevertheless, the economic and competitive situations in each foreign market are different enough that the marketer must understand the variables unique to the local market before being able to set appropriate prices there. We have identified the major variables influencing pricing in those foreign markets where the firm has subsidiaries. We noted how these variables impinge on the pricing process and suggested some approaches marketers might use in managing pricing in the firm's foreign markets.

The last three chapters have discussed the international dimensions of three of the four Ps of marketing: product policy, place or distribution, and pricing. That leaves promotion, which we'll discuss in Chapter 8.

QUESTIONS

1. What are the differences between pricing for export and the firm's pricing within foreign markets?

2. What factors influence the relationship between a firm's domestic prices and its export prices?
3. Explain the phenomenon of price escalation in exporting.
4. How can firms deal with the problem of price escalation?
5. Discuss the considerations in choosing between the seller's currency and the buyers' currency for export price quotes.
6. Why is C.I.F. pricing recommended over an ex-factory price quote?
7. Discuss the role of government in pricing within foreign markets.
8. How is pricing within a foreign market similar to—and different from—pricing within the domestic market?
9. Discuss the problems of pricing in highly inflationary economies.

FURTHER READING

1. Feinschreiber, Robert, *Transfer Pricing Handbook*, 2nd ed. (New York: J. Wiley, 1998).
2. Jain, Subhash C., *International Marketing Management*, 5th ed. (Cincinnati, OH: South-Western College Publishing, 1996), Chapter 13.
3. Pasternak, Volker, "The Right Price: China's New Price Law," *Chinese Business Review* vol. 25, no. 5 (September–October 1998), pp. 40–44.
4. Samli, A. Coskun, and Laurence Jacobs, "Pricing Practices of American Multinational Firms: Standardization vs. Localization," *Journal of Global Marketing* vol. 8, no. 2 (1994), pp. 51–73.
5. Terpstra, Vern, and Ravi Sarathy, *International Marketing*, 7th ed. (Fort Worth, TX: Dryden Press, 1997), Chapters 14 and 15.
6. *Transnational Corporations: Transfer Pricing and Taxation*, Sylvain Plasschaert and John H. Dunning, eds. (New York: Routledge, 1994).

NOTE: Basic marketing texts cover the various dimensions of pricing in domestic marketing.

International Dimensions of Promotion

Promotion is that part of the marketing mix through which the firm most directly communicates with its customers. Some communication takes place via the firm's product, pricing, and distribution policies, but the firm relies primarily on its promotional activities to get its message to the market. That message may take many different forms, from a singing commercial to a sales brochure to a technical engineering presentation, but the objective is the same, to persuade the customer to buy the firm's product or service. Thus, while promotional messages carry information of interest to the customer, their role for the marketer is persuasion. Even though firms engage in many different activities to persuade customers to buy their product, the most widely used promotional tools are advertising and personal selling. We shall look at the international dimensions of these forms of promotion.

ADVERTISING IN FOREIGN MARKETS

Note that our topic is "advertising in foreign markets," not "international advertising." We make this distinction because most advertising is not truly international in the sense that it crosses national borders. Most

BOX 8-1   *What's Wrong with This Picture?*

A beautiful woman, dressed in a clingy black, nearly backless formal gown, looks over her right shoulder. She's eating an ice cream cone; Ben and Jerry's new macadamia nut double chocolate fudge. The intent of the message is to have Ben and Jerry's consumers associate their ice cream with the idea that it is luxurious, decadent, and enjoyed by the elite.

What's wrong with this picture? Nothing as long as it's not used in Kuwait, Saudi Arabia, or Afghanistan. Any sort of nudity is forbidden and the backless gown, naked arms, and uncovered hair is just too much sex. Eating the ice cream cone is also too suggestive.

Calvin Klein and Versace change their advertising for some markets by taking models out of the ads, or they must crop or black-out the offending parts of the body from the advertisements. What is a marketer to do? Armani and Gucci develop different ads for these markets, often showing the product or the name of the designer as the focal point. The advertisements can be created at the same time by shooting a few extra frames of background, without the models, and then adding the name or picture of the product in the editing room. Most realize that some adaptation is necessary, even when a standardized or global strategy is appropriate.

In Taiwan, Kate Moss is not welcome. She's too skinny and unhealthy looking. The animal rights groups in England had won a ban for a Levi's ad that showed a hamster die at the end of the commercial. French Connection, a clothing retailer decided to use the controversy caused by its ads to boost sales. They received complaints from British customers that the name of the company's private label, FCUK was too offensive. In response, the firm added the name to the front of its tee shirts and prominently displayed the name on other clothing items. From the United States, the Body Shop had to remove ads from their stores that showed a near naked man with a bottle of self-tanning lotion stuffed in the front of his very tiny briefs with the copy, "just fake it."

One jeans manufacturer, Diesel is known for its outrageous ads. The firm did not use the grandma grabbing grandpa's crotch ad in the Middle East, but it has made a few mistakes. In promoting its ine of stonewashed jeans in Argentina, Diesel showed models chained to stones floating in the water. This offended Argentineans because this is one way the desaparecidos (the people who disappeared during the junta's rule) were out to death. Diesel also ran afoul in Turkey by showing mating horses, one black, the other white. Unfortunately, in Turkey a black horse is the symbol used by one political party, and the white by an opposing party. Even though they received hundreds of protest letters, mostly from angry clerics who denounced the ad as sacrilegious, Diesel did not remove its ad which showed nuns reciting the rosary before Madonna, all were clad in jeans. In general, most advertisers have learned that religion, sex, and politics are topics that require special care when used as promotional themes.

Source: Women's Wear Daily (WWD), February 5, 1999, 12.

EXHIBIT 8-1   *Some Barriers to Advertising Communication*
in International Marketing

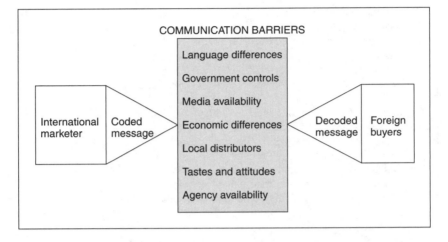

advertising is produced and consumed within national markets. This does not mean that international marketers do not coordinate their advertising abroad. Indeed, they will almost always add an international dimension to such advertising, and one will often find strong similarities from country to country. It does mean, however, that national market characteristics will constrain the firm's advertising in individual countries. Before looking at the advertising task of the international marketer, therefore, we must identify some of the national variables affecting that task.

Exhibit 8-1 illustrates some of the problems facing the international advertiser. A seller in one country wants to send persuasive messages to potential buyers in other countries. Assuring effective communication is challenging enough when the seller and buyer are in the same country. When seller and buyer are in different countries and cultures, many extra barriers to advertising communication must be considered. Here we discuss a number of these differences facing the international advertiser.

THE NATIONAL ENVIRONMENT OF ADVERTISING

The Importance of Advertising within the Country

The economic and cultural role of advertising varies significantly from country to country. Some indication of the varying economic importance of advertising can be seen in Exhibit 8-2 showing advertising as a percentage of gross national product in selected countries. The heavy advertisers in the first column are primarily the rich industrialized countries, those most like the United States. The presence of Argentina and Taiwan on that list suggests that income and industrialization alone are not sufficient indicators of the role of advertising in a nation. Countries in the second set of columns are those in which advertising plays a smaller role. For the most part, these are developing countries, and Asia, Africa, and the Middle East predominate among the light advertisers.

Exhibit 8-2 suggests that a nation's level of economic development is a good general indicator of the role advertising will play. Income alone does not explain the role of advertising, however, because some relatively poor countries are heavy advertisers, and some relatively rich countries are light advertisers, such as Belgium. This discrepancy suggests that other cultural variables must be considered in seeking to understand the role of advertising. *Religion* is one such variable. For example, Buddhism stresses the absence of desire as a virtue. Advertisers generally seek to raise the level of desire. Muslim countries are reluctant to accept many

EXHIBIT 8-2   *Advertising as a Percentage of GNP for Selected Countries*

Heavy Advertisers		Light Advertisers	
Country	Percent of GNP	Country	Percent of GNP
United States	2.30	Ecuador	.001
New Zealand	1.61	Chile	.002
Greece	1.60	Colombia	.002
Argentina	1.59	Venezuela	.008
South Korea	1.41	Mexico	.131
United Kingdom	1.38	Pakistan	.214
Taiwan	1.31	India	.255
Australia	1.27	Indonesia	.307
Israel	1.20	Portugal	.364
Netherlands	1.18	Turkey	.404
Japan	1.13	Philippines	.495
Germany	1.00	Belgium	.554

Sources: *International Marketing Data and Statistics 1998*, 22nd ed. (London: Euromonitor Plc, 1998); *European Marketing Data and Statistics 1998*, 33rd ed. (London: Euromonitor Plc, 1998).

western innovations, innovations that are mostly from "Christian" nations. This resistance is especially noticeable in those countries with large populations of conservative Muslims, such as Afghanistan, Pakistan, Malaysia, and Tajikistan.

Literacy is another constraint on advertising. Low literacy rates in a country make it difficult to advertise in print media. Furthermore, some of these countries have no commercial radio or TV, which would be a way of reaching illiterate as well as literate consumers. *Linguistic diversity is* another problem. A multiplicity of languages within a country makes for diseconomies of scale and high advertising costs. A multiple-language environment is a great handicap to an advertiser. The country of Congo illustrates the problem at its worst.

> The Democratic Republic of the Congo has a population of about 45 million. The official language is French, but only a small fraction of the population speaks French. Four lingua francas cover most of the country with about one-fourth of the population for each of these language bridges. Most of the people, however, are most comfortable and conversant in their own tribal languages. The more than one hundred of these tribal languages are mostly mutually incomprehensible. These tribal languages would be the best medium for the persuasive communications of the advertiser, but preparing advertising in any number of them would be an insurmountable task.

Promotional Infrastructure

A firm's ability to advertise in a country will be affected by the supporting infrastructure available there. Within the United States, the infrastructure for advertising includes many marketing research sources and firms, and many advertising agencies to help with the job. An extensive array of communications media is available to choose from: mail, newspapers, magazines, radio, television, billboards, and more. As one goes down the scale of economic development, various parts of this infrastructure are missing or inadequate. Mail service, for example, is an occasional occurrence in the large rural areas of developing countries. Many nations have no reliable figures on the circulation or audience of the various media. Television coverage is limited in a number of developing countries, and even in some affluent countries. Recent data show that in Israel, television advertising accounted for only 6.0 percent of total ad dollars spent, and in Switzerland the amount spent on TV ads was only 8.9 percent.

National regulations and *different media availability* can force an advertiser to modify a promotional program.

China is allowing advertising to be included on video compact discs in order to make the programs more affordable for the people of China. The 2-minute ads are expected to reduce the price of the average compact disc by 40 percent (from the current price of $2.80 to $1.80). A by-product of cheaper discs is lower piracy rates; Chinese will have less incentive to illegally copy the discs.

Campaigns prepared for television and/or radio will not be quite the same as those for print media. Exhibit 8-3 indicates the relative importance of various media in several countries. The role of print media ranges from 5 percent to 80 percent, with wide ranges also for television and other media. Radio's share goes from 1 percent in Denmark to more than 18 percent in the Colombia. It should be noted, however, that the trend in most countries is for a greater role for commercial television at the expense of radio and print media. This change is largely due to the growing number of TV viewers, but it is also partly

EXHIBIT 8-3   *Percent of Total Advertising Expenditures by Media*

| Country | Media | | | |
	TV (%)	Print (%)	Radio (%)	Other (%)
Brazil	59.0	34.0	4.0	3.0
Canada	26.7	50.2	11.8	11.3
Colombia	61.2	20.2	18.6	0.0
Czech Republic	36.2	45.3	7.3	11.2
Denmark	22.5	73.9	1.3	2.3
Germany	18.8	73.0	3.6	4.6
India	20.8	67.4	2.9	8.9
Israel	6.0	80.4	4.4	9.2
Italy	53.4	39.5	3.6	3.5
Japan	46.6	40.4	5.3	8.2
Netherlands	18.6	66.0	3.0	12.4
Peru	88.7	5.2	6.2	0.0
Philippines	65.4	18.5	15.3	0.8
Sweden	23.9	68.5	2.3	0.6
United States	55.5	39.4	3.5	1.7

Sources: *International Marketing Data and Statistics 1998*, 22nd ed. (London: Euromonitor Plc, 1998); *European Marketing Data and Statistics 1998*, 33rd ed. (London: Euromonitor Plc, 1998).

due to governments' desire to reduce the expense of public telecasting. Also, a political dimension influences media selection in countries where media may be associated with particular political viewpoints or parties.

> In Colombia, advertising in *El Tiempo* and not in *Espectador* could cause trouble for an advertiser. These two leading papers support rival political factions and reach different audiences. Advertising campaigns generally must be placed in both newspapers.

Advertising agencies are a critical element in the promotional infrastructure of a country, and their nature and availability vary significantly around the world. The rich industrialized countries generally have many agencies with a number offering full service, just as the U.S. firm is accustomed to at home. As the firm goes into poorer economies and smaller markets, both the number of agencies and the calibre of service tend to decline. For example, the United Kingdom has more than 600 agencies, and Sweden has more than 160, a number of which are full-service agencies. By contrast, countries such as Cambodia, Ghana, and Zambia have only a few agencies. Indeed, as of 1998, 14 countries had only one major agency. In these smaller, poorer markets, the firm will frequently have to go without *some* of the agency services it uses elsewhere. The multinational firm will often play the role of educator in the fledgling local agency, helping it to upgrade so it can offer better service in the future. This educational process takes place by working with agency staff, supplying materials from more advanced markets, and, occasionally, sending agency personnel to the home office or the home agency.

Government and Advertising

The U.S. government does not practice laissez-faire with respect to advertising, but its involvement is not heavy enough to warrant much consideration in advertising discussion. Abroad, some countries have tighter restrictions and others have lighter restrictions than the United States. One major constraint, already noted, is that a number of countries do not allow advertising on radio and/or television. Another constraint for some firms is that governments usually regulate advertising for cigarettes, liquor, and a variety of other products considered sensitive.

> On January 1, 1998, a ban on tobacco advertising on all commercial radio and television stations took effect in Estonia.

After nearly a decade, the European Union has adopted stricter advertising guidelines for tobacco products. By October 1, 2006, all tobacco advertising and sponsorships will be illegal.

The World Health Organization, in launching its "No Tobacco Day" on May 31, 1998, called for a worldwide ban on all tobacco advertising.

In January of 1999, a controversial bill banning all advertising and promotion of tobacco products, as well as outlawing smoking in public and in private residences was being debated in the South African Parliament.

Some countries have requirements stipulating which languages may be used for advertising, and others require some kinds of ads to be prepared locally, rather than in the firm's home office. Twenty-four countries have mandatory government preclearance of commercials for certain product categories. New Zealand, a country of 3.6 million people, has no less than 33 different laws that relate to advertising. Taxes are another kind of government control in some countries. Sweden, for example, taxes newspaper ads at 6 percent and other media at 10 percent, whereas in England, newspaper and magazine ads are not taxed at all, while other media ads pay 8 percent tax. A broader kind of challenge to advertising occurs when government appears to attack the institution of advertising itself.

The British government attacked Procter & Gamble and Unilever for the volume of their detergent advertising, which it claimed raised the price of the product.

On similar grounds, India challenged Firestone and other tire companies for their advertising expenditures.

Indonesia's government introduced rules restricting newspapers from having more than 30 percent of their space in advertising. Previously, up to 50 percent of the space was occupied by ads. Television advertising is also restricted. Advertising agencies claim that the national consumer board wants to eliminate advertising entirely.

ADVERTISING IN EXPORT AND LICENSEE MARKETS

In countries where the firm sells through independent distributors or licensees, these parties will handle the marketing and advertising of the firm's products in their markets. In such cases the international marketer will have no advertising task in such markets, beyond sending copies of advertising materials used by the firm in other countries. Such a laissez-faire approach may be necessary where distributors and licensees do not want any help (or interference) from the exporter or licensor. This hands-off approach may even be desirable in many cases. After all, distributors and licensees know their own market best; it is usually in their self-interest to promote the product well; and they get cheaper local rates in the media. If they are good marketers, they can probably do the job better than their foreign supplier.

Many exporters and licensors do leave the foreign marketing and advertising in the hands of their distributors and licensees. They do so sometimes because of the advantages already noted, but frequently it is the result of inadequate staff, inexperience, and lack of expertise on the part of the exporter or licensor. Often, the exporting-licensing firm could get more effective foreign advertising and marketing if it played a more active role. However, this task requires experienced personnel who may not be found in many smaller exporting or licensing firms. Whenever the international firm is a more sophisticated marketer than its distributors and licensees, it should try to play some role in its foreign advertising and marketing. At the least, the firm should have greater expertise in the promotion of its own products, especially when distributors handle a wide range of products and have no special knowledge of many parts of their product line.

Larger, more experienced exporters and licensors generally try to have some role in the promotional efforts of their distributors-licensees. But, if it is the distributor's or licensee's responsibility, why should the international marketer get involved? International firms undertake what appears to be an extra task for several reasons.

1. Distributors-licensees might not voluntarily be giving any advertising support to the firm's products.
2. They may be advertising, but in a way the firm considers ineffective or even prejudicial.
3. Distributor-licensee advertising might be widely inconsistent from country to country, and the firm wants a more uniform image and positioning.
4. For legal reasons, the firm may find it necessary to control closely the claims made by its foreign representatives, especially in the case of pharmaceuticals and other products affecting life and safety.

If the international marketing firm decides to get involved in advertising in distributor-licensee markets, some kind of cooperative program needs to be established with the distributors or licensees. The firm could, of course, conduct its own advertising in such markets without involving its local representatives. When that is done, the distributor-licensee markets are treated more like subsidiary markets. We will discuss such advertising in the next section on subsidiary markets. *Here, we will look at the issues involved in cooperative advertising with distributors and licensees.* The major issues relate to the division of labor in cooperative advertising: Who does what in regard to paying for the advertising, choosing the message, and selecting the media and the advertising agency? How is cooperative advertising controlled in many far-flung markets?

Cooperative Advertising

Payment

Payment for cooperative advertising is usually divided equally between the local and international firms. The international firm occasionally will pay more than half to ensure effective advertising and in situations in which the distributor is unable or unwilling to pay 50 percent. The exporter-licensor hopes that more advertising will be done with a cooperative program. If the international firm's money is merely substituted for that of the local firm, a cooperative program is less interesting. It may still be worthwhile, however, if it leads to more effective advertising and increased sales. Another advantage may come from the cooperative approach when the local partner gets more favorable media rates than would be available to a foreign firm.

Message

The international firm likes to play a major role in the selection of the advertising message. That message is often the major variable in determining the success of advertising, and the international firm has more experience in this area. The firm will draw on its experience in its domestic market and other international markets. Even though the messages will not necessarily be the same in every country, they will be more similar in a cooperative program. Beyond increased effectiveness, the benefits are reduced creative costs and more uniform appeals and positioning from country to country. Effective coordination facilitates the task of the international marketer.

Media and Agency

Media selection is ordinarily left to the national firm because of its local knowledge. *Selection of the advertising agency* is of greater interest to international firms. Because they frequently use multinational agencies, they would like to use the same agency in every country insofar as possible. The use of such an agency minimizes their communications problems and administrative costs, and facilitates control of the cooperative advertising program. The local branch of the multinational agency acts on behalf of its international client. Sometimes, however, the distributor or licensee is unwilling to disturb its ties to a local agency. Then the international firm may have to accept the local agency instead of its own choice, even though the local agency better represents the distributor or licensee than it does the international firm.

Control

Controlling cooperative advertising involves assuring, for distant foreign markets, that the *right ads* have been *properly placed* and that *payment* has been made according to the agreement. It is a long-distance policing job. As indicated earlier, the job is much easier if the international firm has a branch of its multinational agency in the country concerned. Otherwise it requires visits by the international marketer and/or tear-sheets and invoices from the local firm. Occasionally horror stories surface about the local firm sending bogus invoices and pocketing the money without running the ads. Control problems are inversely related to the calibre of the local distributor or licensee, emphasizing again the importance of selecting the right partner in the first place.

> When Pepsico wanted to accelerate its campaign to catch up with Coca-Cola overseas, it called its first international convention. Pepsico gathered all its bottler-distributors from all over the globe to a meeting (pep rally) in Los Angeles to enlist them in a greater cooperative effort in marketing Pepsi-Cola in their markets. Pepsi issued a manual on advertising graphics and launched the Pepsi-Cola International Management Institute.

ADVERTISING IN FOREIGN SUBSIDIARY MARKETS

Advertising in countries where the firm has a subsidiary is a task similar to the one faced in the home market. The firm is physically present in those markets, and the basic job of advertising is the same everywhere: the right message in the right media at the right time. Differences are inevitable, of course, in the firm's advertising from country to country because of the unique environmental variables in each market and because of differing competition and company situations, such as volume of business, product line, media, and market share in each country. Media availability is also a factor, for example, access to the Internet. Nevertheless, the subsidiary has the job of domestic advertising in its local market, just as the parent company does at home. This essential similarity allows us to confine ourselves to the two areas in which the international dimension is most prominent: choosing the advertising agency and choosing the message.

BOX 8-2   *The Internet as an Advertising Medium*

In order to drive down distribution costs, increase exposure, and have more direct contact with its consumers, firms are using the Internet for e-commerce. On the revenue side, the Internet is also beginning to generate advertising dollars.

Estimates of worldwide online advertising for 1999 exceed $5 billion, with the United States contributing almost half of this ad revenue. The advertising agency Dentsu reported that in 1998, online advertising of Japanese products grew nearly 90 percent over the previous year to $100 million and by the end of 1999, spending is anticipated to reach $170 million. The Internet research firm Datamonitor expects European ad spending to grow from $180 million in 1998 to nearly $2 billion by 2003.

According to the global Internet Advertising Bureau, in 1999 the global ad spending for consumer goods, which accounted for 27 percent of ad revenue, exceeded spending for computers and related products, which was 24 percent. Financial services accounted for 16 percent of ad revenue, followed by telecommunications products at 11 percent.

The goal of the Internet Advertising Bureau (IAB) is to bring some direction to the medium by recommending standards, conducting and sponsoring research, and educating the advertising industry and users about the effectiveness of Internet advertising.

The Internet is an advertising medium in its infancy. The medium is gaining widespread accepted among firms and their customers, and its use is growing exponentially. The question is, how long before it replaces print as the #1 advertising medium?

Sources: "Online Advertising Expected to Grow Rapidly, Diversify," Technology Briefs, *Philadelphia Inquirer*, (March 18, 1999) <http://www.phillynews.com/inquirer/>; "Internet Ad Sales Nearly Double in Japan," *Advertising Age International* <http://adage.com/international/daily/index.com>; Internet Advertising Bureau home page <http://www.iab.net/>; The Internet Local Advertising and Commerce Association home page <http://www.ilac.net>.

Choosing an Advertising Agency

Advertising is one marketing function that the firm usually hires from an outside specialist, the advertising agency. This outsourcing is practiced

EXHIBIT 8-4   *Leading Multinational Advertising Agencies*

Ad Organization	Headquarters	Gross Income (US$ Millions)
Omnicom Group	New York	$4,154.3
WPP Group	London	3,646.6
Interpublic Group	New York	3,384.5
Dentsu	Tokyo	1,987.8
Young & Rubicam	New York	1,497.9
True North Comm.	Chicago	1,211.5
Grey Advertising	New York	1,143.0
Havas Advertising	Paris	1,033.1
Leo Burnett Co.	Chicago	878.0
Hakuhodo	Tokyo	848.0

Source: *Ad Age Dataplace,* <http://adage.com/dataplace>.

abroad as well as at home, so in all markets, the choice of an advertising agency is one of the most important variables in the success of an advertising program. Availability of media varies from market to market, as discussed earlier, and technological developments offer new advertising opportunities. Additionally, in foreign markets the advertising agency acts as a cultural bridge between the international firm and the local market. Two principal alternatives are open to the firm when choosing an agency for a foreign market. It can choose a different national agency for each market, or it can choose the local office of a multinational agency. The giant multinational agencies, many of which are U.S. companies, have offices in a number of major markets. The largest agencies, with over $1 billion in annual revenues, have offices in many countries (see Exhibit 8-4). Technological advances and industry trends provide many alternatives.

Strategic alliances among advertising agencies are being formed to offer the latest innovations. Interactive or smart commercials, digital TV, e-commerce, the Intercast, WebTV, and WaveTop broadcasts are ushering in new ways of promoting products and interacting with consumers. Agency.com, a U.S.–based company, which is in partly owned by Omnicom, merged with Spiral Media and Interactive solutions, both also U.S.–based, and the leading online service agency in the United Kingdom, Online Magic. Their new arm, dubbed iTV is developing interactive ad campaigns for their multinational clients, which include British Air, American Express, and Unilever.

The proper choice of an agency for a foreign market will depend on how the needs and objectives of the firm relate to what the candidate agencies have to offer. We shall discuss some of the considerations involved in choosing between an independent local agency and the local branch of a multinational agency.

The Local Agency

An independent advertising agency in a foreign market might be a good choice if it is the *most effective agency available*. If advertising is important in the marketing mix and the firm is therefore dependent on good advertising, it may find that a national agency can do the best job. If the international firm wishes to have a *national image* rather than a foreign or international image, it will often choose a national agency. For example, IBM used national agencies in its foreign markets to further its image as a good local citizen. If the multinational firm is decentralized and offers a lot of *autonomy to foreign subsidiaries* as profit centers, the choice of an advertising agency is frequently left to the subsidiaries, and they will often choose a national agency. Apart from its effect on the advertising program, giving the subsidiary the freedom to choose the agency is important for subsidiary morale. Finally, if the international firm uses *localized advertising campaigns*, tailored to each market rather than internationally coordinated, a national agency can serve as well as a multinational agency office.

The Multinational Agency

The multinational agencies' share of world advertising has grown steadily, because of the demand for their services, especially by multinational company clients. Several considerations might favor the firm's foreign subsidiary choosing the local office of a multinational agency, rather than an independent national agency.

1. When the multinational firm wants relatively *standardized appeals and positioning* around the world, it will find the task much easier to achieve if it can deal with one international agency whose foreign market coverage approximates its own network of subsidiaries, rather than dealing with a number of independent agencies. The firm's subsidiaries tend to be in the larger foreign markets as are the branches of the multinational agencies.

2. When multinational firms want to exercise some central control over their international advertising (as they generally do), it can greatly reduce its *administrative and communications costs* if it can deal with a single agency group. The agency group works with the firm in controlling the advertising program on an international basis.

3. When the multinational firm has a *limited volume of business* in certain markets, it may have an advertising budget too small to call forth the best efforts of independent national agencies. If a multinational agency handles a number of the firm's markets, both large and small, the total advertising budget is sufficient to encourage good service, even in smaller markets.

4. When the multinational firm wants to advertise in *distributor and licensee markets* without having a cooperative program there, it will find the use of a multinational agency imperative. It is especially difficult and expensive to deal with separate national agencies in markets where the firm has no personal presence. By contrast, the local offices of the multinational agency can act as the firm's representative in distributor and licensee markets, making control of advertising there both feasible and economic.

5. When a multinational firm chooses the local office of a multinational agency, it does not have to worry that it is sacrificing quality or local knowledge. The local branches of multinational agencies are often among the best agencies in their markets and have either been there for many years or represent an acquisition of an established local agency.

As mentioned, large multinational agencies may take different approaches depending on their clients' needs:

Saab AB unveiled its new advertising strategy. The objectives are to promote the concept that their cars defy convention, and by focusing on its roots as an aircraft manufacturer, emphasize the sleek design, safety, and power of the automobiles. Another objective is to develop this unified image worldwide. The company developed a central theme for its advertisements worldwide—referred to as the "Saab versus" ads. For example, the "Saab versus the police" ads exalt the antitheft protection. Saab produced a number of add-ins from locations around the world, and are encouraging local Saab managers to choose from this inventory. So, while the theme of the advertisements are the same, they are adapted to local markets.

The New York Agency of D'Arcy Masius Benton & Bowles is reorganizing to better offer global strategies for its multinational clients. Teams consisting of account directors, creative directors, and account planners will now have global responsibility for campaigns that are worldwide in scope. For example, plans call for a single ad campaign for Proctor & Gamble's Charmin brand toilet tissue for Germany, France, the United Kingdom, Hong Kong, South Korea, and Mexico.

Choosing the Message

Advertising messages are the principal means of communication between the producer and the consumer. They play an important but lesser role in industrial marketing. Finding the right message is one of the most critical aspects of an advertising program. It is wasteful, even counterproductive, to spend a lot of money on media if the message is ineffective. Knowing that each foreign market is unique in many respects, we might expect that the best message for a market is one that is custom-designed for that market. It would be surprising then to find a great deal of similarity in the advertising messages of a multinational firm in different countries. One of the continuing debates in this field is the question of how standardized international advertising can or should be. Looking at that debate provides a useful way to guide the selection of appropriate advertising messages in foreign markets.

Localized Messages

Favoring localized messages are the advertising personnel in the subsidiary and the independent national agency. Their importance is enhanced to the degree that their market is considered different from the other markets of the firm. If their market were not unique, presumably their job could be largely done at international headquarters. Beyond these subjective considerations, other factors favor localized messages. The most important one, of course, is when *local buying motives* are indeed different from those elsewhere. To the degree that this differentiation is true, a message borrowed from another market would not be effective. *Differing media availability* can encourage localized campaigns. TV is a major medium in some markets but not available in others. The differing requirements of print media may cause a change in the advertising message in those countries where the firm must use print media instead of TV.

Those firms that choose to employ independent *national advertising agencies* in foreign markets are more likely to use localized campaigns. Indeed, it is difficult to have standardized advertising when a different agency is used in each market. Multinationals that have *decentralized marketing and advertising* down to the subsidiary level are also likely to have localized advertising. Subsidiaries in different countries preparing their advertising program will generally tailor it to their local market in the absence of headquarters' requests for international coordination. In other words, internationalization of advertising doesn't happen without conscious effort.

> Hewlett-Packard (HP) is somewhat unusual as a high-tech company that doesn't formally centralize its international advertising. Most advertising decisions are delegated to overseas subsidiaries, which are encouraged to consider local personalities, business trends, and cultural preferences in planning advertising programs. Generally, ads for HP products in other countries are not similar to those created in the United States.

International Messages

Firms seldom have identical advertising in all their markets, but often show great similarity across countries. Several reasons explain this similarity. The use of a *multinational advertising agency* encourages standardized advertising because one of their selling points is their ability to manage such campaigns. A *desire for headquarters control* of international advertising encourages standardized campaigns. The headquarters advertising department is more important if it runs the whole show than if each subsidiary does its own thing. Apart from these subjective considerations, stronger reasons may exist for headquarters control. For example, if the firm wants a *uniform product image and positioning* across markets, it will pursue greater international standardization. Revlon is an example of such a company. For this reason, Revlon prepares ads centrally and allows field managers to revise them only with headquarters approval.

One of the most important reasons for internationally similar advertising is the *international similarity of buying motives* for certain kinds of products. Such diverse firms as Revlon, Coca-Cola, and Exxon claim to find such similarity. *Economic benefits* can also be realized from internationalized advertising. Some economies arise from the improved coordination, control, and evaluation that is possible with more standardized advertising. Other economies can come from the extension to new markets of ideas and techniques proven successful elsewhere. It is part of the synergy available to multinationals. Money put into research and creative work has a higher payoff when it can be applied in many countries.

Intel began advertising in 1986 to differentiate the company's products from competitors such as Cyrix. The Intel logo and "Intel Inside" slogan are recognizable internationally. Intel also took a global approach to promoting its latest chip technologies. The dancing techies, clad in bright metallic clean suits are traveling the globe in their Intel-mobile. These characters appear in various media in the United States, Asia, the United Kingdom, Germany, Poland, and the Czech Republic. They are being beamed into homes via pan-European programming including MTV and Eurosport too. As they travel the world, adaptation for ethnic and physiological differences is not necessary since the characters are neither gender- nor ethnic-specific. The dancing techies are a great international symbol.

In concluding this discussion, we must note that the appropriate advertising message for a foreign market will be determined by research and experience in that market. The effectiveness of advertising will be decided in the market place, not by debating pros and cons. For some products and some countries, advertising messages will be relatively localized. For other products or countries, a high degree of standardization may be feasible, even advantageous. The multinational firm will determine the proper approach with the help of its advertising agency. In the global village in which we are living, however, it is probable that most firms will find some degree of central coordination of advertising both feasible and profitable, just as we see more pan-European advertising as in the Intel example.

PERSONAL SELLING

In contrast to the impersonal messages of advertising, personal selling conveys information and persuasive messages through individual personal contact. Though it is less visible than advertising, which comes into our homes and automobiles, personal selling is even more important in terms of the budget allocated to it. U.S. firms spend about three times as much money on personal selling as on advertising. For several reasons, personal selling sometimes plays an even greater role in markets abroad than domestically. Low literacy rates, government restrictions on advertising, and lack of media availability can limit the amount of advertising the firm can do, emphasizing the importance of the alternative: personal selling. Furthermore, low wage rates in developing countries make personal selling a relatively cheap form of promotion there.

For consumer goods marketers, personal selling generally means selling to intermediaries, such as wholesalers and retailers, rather than to the ultimate consumer. Exceptions in the United States are firms such as Avon, Tupperware, Firestone, and Singer. Somewhat surprisingly, all of these companies have successfully used their same direct selling techniques in foreign markets. For industrial marketers, personal selling often means selling to the final customer, as with IBM computer marketing. In foreign markets, personal selling usually plays the same role as at home. One difference is that in many countries, thin markets and/or a fragmented wholesale-retail structure may limit the amount of direct selling that can be done profitably. As noted in the chapter on retailing, even in Japan, General Foods had to join with a large Japanese firm in order to sell directly to retailers.

Personal selling is largely a national phenomenon. Little is done across national boundaries. Indeed, much is done on a regional or subnational level because linguistic, ethnic, or religious differences segment many countries' markets. As in the case of advertising, personal selling in distributor and licensee markets will be handled by the distributors and licensees. Similarly, some inputs may come from the international firm. In the countries where the firm has a subsidiary, it has the same sales management task as in its home market. Because the *principles* of sales management apply abroad as well as at home, we shall confine our discussion to some international dimensions of the *practice* of sales management in the multinational firm. We use the standard listing of the sales management tasks: recruitment, selection, training, motivation, compensation, supervision, and evaluation of the salesforce, as shown in Exhibit 8-5.

Recruitment and Selection

Recruitment and selection of a salesforce in any country are constrained by certain national peculiarities. One is the educational system, which may be weak or strong in supplying the kind of people needed for sales work. Another is the attitude toward the vocation of personal selling. In many countries this attitude is negative and makes many otherwise good prospects avoid selling as a career option. A third important factor is the difference in languages, religions, and races within a country, which can make it difficult, if not counterproductive, for a salesperson of one group to try to sell to members of another group. For these reasons, the international firm must leave recruitment and selection of the salesforce primarily to subsidiary management who are acquainted with the peculiarities of their own market.

EXHIBIT 8-5   *The Task of Salesforce Management*

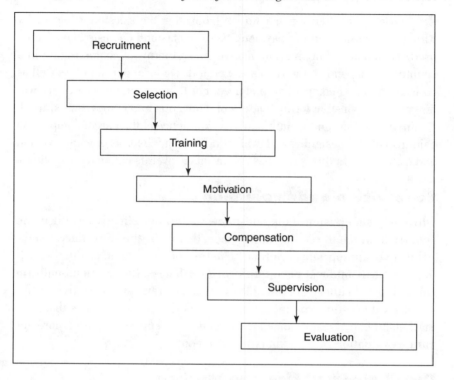

Training

In the area of training, the multinational firm will be able to make the greatest contribution to its subsidiary's sales management task. The multinational has a repository of experience in sales management, not only in its domestic market, but also in a number of foreign markets. Based on this experience, the multinational knows more about the effectiveness of different kinds of training programs and techniques. The subsidiary can draw on this experience in designing sales training programs appropriate to its own market. Other benefits include its ability to draw on headquarters experts for short-term training programs, such as for new product introductions. Sales personnel from several subsidiaries in a geographic region can be trained together. This method provides economies of scale and is more attractive to the salesforce than a one-country program. In certain cases, sales personnel may be sent to the parent company for training programs. This method again offers economies and is a morale booster.

Motivation and Compensation

Compensation is often a major way of motivating the salesforce, especially with a commission form of payment. Sales quotas and contests may also be used. The choice of appropriate motivators and forms of compensation in a country will depend on the values and attitudes of local personnel, as well as on local laws and competitive practices. For this reason, the subsidiary will be largely responsible for the pattern of motivation and compensation used. Again, it can draw on the multinational experience of the parent company to gain insights for designing and evaluating alternative forms of compensation and motivation. In this way, it has an advantage over its national competitors.

Supervision and Evaluation

Obviously, supervision of the salesforce can be done effectively only in the country in which the selling takes place, that is, by the subsidiary. Establishment of appropriate performance norms for control and evaluation will depend partly on local peculiarities. Nevertheless, the international firm can aid its subsidiary in both of these tasks. Through comparative analysis of its domestic experience and its experience in similar subsidiary markets, it can give guidance for more effective supervision and more accurate evaluation by subsidiary management.

Distributor and Licensee Markets

Distributors and licensees are responsible for marketing—including personal selling—in their markets. Many times, however, the international firm can and will aid them in their marketing as in the ease of cooperative advertising. Frequently, the international marketer will supply distributors and licensees with the same *sales promotional materials* given to the salesforce in the firm's subsidiaries. Sometimes the multinational firm will even give the distributors' and licensees' salesforces the same *training programs* given to its own subsidiary sales staff. For example, Unisys trains its distributors' salespeople along with its own subsidiary salespeople. They do this at regional locations, say Latin America, for new product introductions.

Review of Personal Selling

Personal selling is done within the foreign market, and management of the salesforce will be done by subsidiary management in their own country.

What we have noted, however, is that both the subsidiary and the multinational firm benefit from the firm's international experience. The subsidiary can be more effective by drawing on its experience as well as the firm's experience in other countries. The subsidiary also benefits from the parent firm's economies of scale. The parent firm enjoys scale economies in training programs and preparing sales materials, contests, and so forth. For example, Firestone brought all their sales leaders from foreign markets to the United States for a one-week holiday reward. International operations also give the parent firm a broader range of experience than it gets domestically, making it aware of a wider range of alternatives and giving insights as to what works or doesn't work in different circumstances. This added experience aids in coordinating and controlling marketing in foreign subsidiaries and also helps to evaluate more effectively the distributors' and licensees' performance.

OTHER KINDS OF PROMOTION

Advertising and personal selling account for the major part of firms' promotional activity both at home and abroad. Other kinds of international marketing promotion, however, deserve at least a mention to round out the picture of the possibilities available.

Public Relations

Public relations activity is *not* part of the marketing program of the firm, and should not be. It is a fact of life, however, that a firm's sales in any market are related to its public image and acceptance there. That means that the firm's image may help either to persuade or to dissuade potential buyers. Therefore, enlightened public relations programs should help firms to be—and to be perceived as—good citizens and contributors to the host country. Such public relations will be supportive of marketing success there. The importance of public relations to marketing can best be seen when the firm fails in public relations. Then it will face a decline or even disappearance of public acceptance of its products. At worst, it could encounter boycotts or demonstrations, as was the case with Nike shoes in the late 1990s because of the use of sweatshop labor in producing footwear.

Trade Fairs

Overseas trade fairs are a popular and generally effective way to introduce and sell many products abroad. A trade fair is a concentrated exhibition of the products of hundreds of producers. They are held annually and may be a one-industry fair or a general exhibition, such as the Hanover Fair with 5,000 exhibitors in 20 industry categories. Hundreds of trade fairs in scores of countries, even including the People's Republic of China. Because these fairs attract large numbers of potential buyers and/or purchase influencers, the firm that exhibits there finds a concentrated market in which to make sales, locate distributors, and/or keep an eye on the local competition that will also be there. These fairs help many U.S. firms to sell their products abroad; therefore the U.S. government facilitates and encourages participation through a Department of Commerce program.

> The U.S. Department of Commerce (USDOC) trade fair program involves participation in more than 20 expositions a year in industrial and developing countries. The department books a block of space up to 20,000 square feet and divides it up among the participants, which usually number 50 to 70 U.S. firms. Now the USDOC is going high-tech by adding a new dimension to trade shows. By taking advantage of new computer software and hardware, they have led the way in the development of the *virtual trade show*. At a recent show in Mexico City, web pages in Spanish and English furnished information about the exhibitors. The USDOC provided computer terminals where prospective buyers could browse through product descriptions and company information. Users were also encouraged to complete customer profile forms that were later compiled as trade leads and then forwarded to the appropriate U.S. exporter. Virtual trade show space was offered free-of-charge to those that also had booth space, but even for those unable to participate, the charge for an online booth was only $150!

Sales Promotion

Sales promotion includes a number of miscellaneous selling activities such as contests, coupons, sampling, and point-of-purchase materials. Generally, these activities are as popular in other countries as they are in the United States. Indeed, premiums, free samples, and cents-off deals are probably even more popular in developing countries where discretionary income is less. European countries have a lot of sales promotional activity, but they regulate it more than does the United States. For example, Radio Shack gave away free flashlights in connection with a promotion in

Germany. They ran into trouble with the government's restrictions on the use of premiums. Radio Shack had done the same thing in U.S. promotions, but the German laws were much stricter on the use of premiums (when, how big, etc.).

> Coupons are among the most popular sales promotion techniques in the United States, Canada, New Zealand, Spain, France, England, and Italy (coupons on some items are restricted in Italy, however). Austria, Germany, and Greece are three EU nations that prohibit the use of coupons. So even with greater harmonization of policies, pan-European promotion runs into some legal obstacles.

The Big Brush

We have indicated some of the major promotional approaches in international marketing. Our brief discussion has not done justice, however, to the colorful mosaic that exists in international promotion. Therefore we will include an example of one company's promotional task in the markets of developing countries—Gillette in Africa and Asia.

> Gillette sells razor blades in most countries of the world but in some places it must first sell the idea of shaving. In some countries, facial hair is removed with a sharp knife, or machete, or a honed edge on a broken soft drink bottle. To persuade these men that shaving can be easier and more comfortable, Gillette has designed a special promotional program, part of which involves "the big brush." Gillette sends a van around from village to village. The van carries "salesmen" and is equipped with washbasins, towels, and razors. Once the salesmen attract a crowd in the village, the big brush is produced and used to lather a volunteer's face with shaving cream. The shaving of the volunteer provides entertainment for the audience. Other villagers are then invited to try out this new form of shaving. This promotional effort is obviously trying to stimulate primary demand for Gillette's kind of shaving. Few sales are made during the campaign itself. For those who are won over, the blades available are the Gillette Blue Blade which is of the generation before the stainless steel blade and several generations before the Trac II, Atra, or Sensor blades.

SUMMARY

Marketers around the world face the task of persuading customers to buy their products or services. They all use the same basic promotional tools— advertising, personal selling, sales promotion—but these tools are used in different ways and to different degrees from one country to another. This chapter has shown some of the common denominators as well as some of the diversity in the promotional task of the international marketer operating in many countries. Diversity provides the challenge in international marketing. We have seen some of the ways firms deal with this challenge: use of international advertising agencies, central coordination, and transfer of experience internationally. The international success of thousands of U.S., European, and Japanese companies shows that the challenges to international promotion can be overcome profitably, if not easily.

QUESTIONS

1. Why does the amount of advertising in different countries around the world vary so widely?
2. How do differing infrastructures (supporting services) affect a firm's ability to advertise in a country?
3. What problems do firms face in advertising in those countries where they are represented by distributors and licensees?
4. Why do multinational firms frequently employ the same advertising agency in many different countries?
5. What reasons often encourage firms to use similar advertising messages from country to country?
6. Why does personal selling often play a bigger role in promotion in other countries than in the United States?
7. What contributions can the multinational firm make to the personal selling activities of its subsidiaries in foreign markets?
8. How can a firm's public relations in a country affect its marketing success there?
9. Discuss the trade fair as a form of promotion in international marketing.

FURTHER READING

1. Church, Nancy, "Advertising in the East Bloc," *Journal of Global Marketing* vol. 5, no. 3 (1992), pp. 109–129.
2. Hill, John S., Richard R. Still, and Unal O. Boya, "Managing the Multinational Sales Force," *International Marketing Review* vol. 8, no. 1 (1991), pp. 19–31.

3. Kirpalani, V.H., *International Advertising: Standardization and Adaptation* (Chicago: American Marketing Association, 1993).
4. Mooij, Marieke K. de, *Advertising Worldwide: Concepts, Theories and Practice of International, Multinational and Global Advertising* (New York: Prentice Hall, 1994).
5. Mueller, Barbara, *International Advertising: Communicating Across Cultures* (Belmont, CA: Wadsworth Publishing, 1996).
6. Rijkens, Rein, European Advertising Strategies: The Profiles and Policies of Multinational Companies Operating in Europe (London: Cassell, 1992).
7. Terpstra, Vern, and Ravi Sarathy, *International Marketing*, 7th ed. (Fort Worth, TX: Dryden Press, 1997), Chapters 12 and 13.

NOTE: Basic marketing texts cover the various aspects of promotion in domestic marketing.

A&P	www.aptea.com
A. C. Nielsen	www.acnielsen.com
Action	www.actionshoes.com
Adidas	www.adidas.com
Agency.com	www.agency.com
American Chamber of Commerce	www.chamber.org
American Express	www.americanexpress.com
AMPAK	www.weldotronco.com/ ampkhmpg.htm
Arthur Andersen Consulting	www.ac.com
Avon	www.avon.com
Bank of America	www.bofa.com
Bata India	www.bata.com
Bata Shoe Co.	www.bata.com
Beach'n Billboard	www.beachnbillboard.com
Boeing	www.boeing.com
Borg-Warner	www.bwsc.com
British Air	www.british-airways.com
British Telecommunications	www.bt.com

Brooks Brothers	www.brooksbrothers.com
Burger King	www.burgerking.com
Business America	www.ita.doc.gov/businessamerica/
Business Week	www.businessweek.com
Campbell Soup Co.	www.campbellsoups.com
CBS Records	www.columbiarecords.com
Chanel	www.chanel.com
Chase Manhattan	www.chase.com
Citicorp	www.citibank.com
Coca-Cola	www.cocacola.com
Colgate-Palmolive	www.colgate.com
College Inn	www.collegeinn.com
Coppernob	www.coppernob.com
Corning	www.corning.com
CPC International	www.bestfoods.com
Crystal International Corporation	www.crystalinternational.com
Culligan	www.culligan-man.com
Cyanamid	www.cyanamid.com
Cyrix	www.cyrix.com
D'Arcy Masius Benton & Bowles	www.dmbb.com
Daiei	www.daiei.co.jp
Dentsu	www.dentsu.co.jp
Deutsche Telekom	www.dtag.de
Digital Equipment	www.digital.com
Disney	www.disney.com
Dow Chemical	www.dow.com
DuPont	www.dupont.com
Eastman Kodak	www.kodak.com
Environmental Proctection Agency	www.epa.gov/
ESOMAR	www.esomar.nl
Evian	www.evian.com
Exxon	www.exxon.com
Fastship Atlantic, Inc.	www.fastshipatlantic.com
Firestone	www.firestone.com
Forbes	www.forbes.com
Ford Motor Co.	www.ford.com
Foremost	www.foremost.com
Fortune	www.fortune.com
France Telecom	www.avenir-telecom.fr

General Dynamics	www.gdeb.com
General Electric	www.ge.com
General Foods	www.kraftfoods.com
General Mills	www.generalmills.com
General Motors	www.gm.com
Gerber Products Co.	www.gerber.com
Gillette	www.gillette.com
Goodyear	www.goodyear.com
Grand Metropolitan	www.grandmet.com
Grey Advertising	www.giworldwide.com
H. J. Heinz	www.heinz.com
Hakuhodo	www.hakuhodo.co.jp
Hamilton Beach	www.hamiltonbeach.com
Havas Advertising	www.havas-advertising.com
Heat Sealing Equipment & Manufacturing Co.	www.weldotronco.com/Inoex.htm
Hewlett-Packard	www.hp.com
HIS	www.his.com
Holiday Inn	www.holiday-inn.com
Honda	www.honda.co.jp/eng
Honeywell	www.honeywell.com
Hyundai	www.hdcorp.co.kr
IDV	www.idv.com
IKEA	www.ikea.com
In-Sink-Erator	www.in-sink-erator.com
Intel	www.intel.com
International Business Machines (IBM)	www.ibm.com
International Chamber of Commerce	www.iccwbo.org
International Monetary Fund (IMF)	www.imf.org
International Telecommunications Union (ITU)	www.itu.org
International Trade Administration	www.ita.doc.gov/
Interpublic Group	www.interpublic.com
Ispat International	www.ispatinternational.com
ITI	www.securitypro.com
Itochu	www.itochu.co.jp
Itoh & Company	www.itohu.co.jp/main/
J. Walter Thompson	www.jwt.com

Johnson & Johnson	www.jnj.com
Kellogg	www.kelloggs.com
Kmart	www.kmart.com
Knorr	www.knorr.com
Kroger	www.kroger.com
Leo Burnett Co.	www.leoburnett.com
Levi Strauss	www.levistrauss.com
LG Semicon	www.lgsemicon.com
Liberty	www.subcontinent.com/1971war/ ads/liberty_ad.html
Lipton	www.lipton.com
Macy's	www.macys.com
Manpower	www.manpower.com
Marks & Spencer	www.marks-and-spencer.com./ asp/mainmen.asp
Matav	www.matav.co.il
Mazda	www.mazda.co.jp
McDonald's	www.mcdonalds.com
McDonnell Douglas	www.mcdonnelldouglas.com
MCI	www.mci.com
Meadowgold	www.meadowgold.com
MediaOne International	www.mediaonegroup.com
Mercedes	www.adtranz.com
Merck	www.merck.com
Micron Technology	www.micron.com
Minnesota Mining & Mfg. (3M)	www.mmm.com
Mitsubishi	www.mitsubishi.co.jp
Mitsui	www.mutsui.co.jp
Mobil	www.mobil.com
Morrison Knudsen	www.mk.com
Muji	www.muji.co.jp
Nabisco	www.rjrnabisco.com
National Organization for Women (NOW)	www.now.org
Nestlé	www.nestle.com
New Covent Garden Soup Co.	www.newcoventgardensoup.com
Nike	info.nike.com
Nissan	www.nissan.co.jp
Nissin	www.nissinfoods.com

Occupational Safety and Health Agency	www.osha.gov/
Océ-Nederland B.V.	www.oce.com
Omnicom Group (now Porter/Novelli)	www.pninternational.com
Organization for Economic Cooperation and Development (OECD)	www.oecd.org
Otis	www.otis.com
PepsiCo	www.pepsico.com
Perrier	www.perrier.com
Pfizer	www.pfizer.com
Philip Morris	ntl.irin.com
Philips	www.philips.com
Pillsbury	www.pillsbury.com
Pitney Bowes	www.pitneybowes.com
Pizza Hut	www.pizzahut.com
Procter & Gamble	www.pg.com
Progresso	www.pillsbury.com/main/ brands/progresso.html
Quaker Oats	www.quakeroats.com
Radio Shack	www.radioshack.com
Reebok International	www.reebok.com
Renault	www.renault.com
Revlon	www.revlon.com
Rio de la Plata	www.bancorio.com.ar
Rolls-Royce	www.rolls-royce.com
S. C. Johnson	www.scjohnsonwax.com
Saab AB	www.saab.com
Safeway	www.safeway.com
Samsung Electronics	www.sec.samsung.co.kr
Sava	www.sava.com
Schick	www.schicktech.com
Sea-Land Service Inc.	www.sealand.com
Sears	www.sears.com
Seibu	www.seibu.co.jp
Seiko	www.seiko-corp.co.jp
Shenandoah Valley Poultry Company	www.shenandoahfoods.com
Sierra Club	www.sierraclub.com
Singer	www.singer-nv.com

Sony	www.sonymusic.com
Strategy Resource (Miami)	www.strategyresources.com
Sumitomo	www.sumitomocorp.co.jp
Swanson	www.swansonfoods.com
Tengelmann	www.tengelmann.de
Texas Instruments	www.ti.com
The Wall Street Journal	www.wsj.com
Toyota	www.toyota.co.jp
Toys'R'Us	www.tru.com
True North Comm.	www.true-north.com
Tupperware	www.tupperware.com
U.N. Food and Agriculture Organization (FAO)	www.fao.org
U.S. Atomic Energy Commission	www.doe.gov/
U.S. Department of Agriculture	www.usda.gov/
U.S. Department of Commerce	www.doc.gov/
U.S. Food and Drug Administration	www.fda.gov/
U.S. Department of Justice	www.usdoj.gov/
U.S. Department of State	www.state.gov/
Unilever	www.unilever.com
Union Bank of Switzerland	www.ubs.com
Union Carbide	www.unioncarbide.com
Unisys	www.unisys.com
United Nations Conference on Trace and Development (UNCTAD)	www.unctad.org
Upjohn (Pharmacia & Upjohn)	www.pharmacia.se
USI (Paramount and Universal Studios)	www.paramount.com
Vanity Fair Corporation	www.vf.com
Volkswagen	www3.vw.com
Wal-Mart	www.wal-mart.com
Warner Lambert	www.warner-lambert.com
World Bank Group (IBRD)	www.worldbank.org
World Health Organization (WHO)	www.who.intl
World Trade Organization	www.wto.org
WorldCom	www.wcom.com
WPP Group	www.wwp.com
Xerox	www.xerox.com
Young & Rubicam	www.yr.com

Index